STEP Into DESTINY

Published by XP Publishing
A department of Christian Services Association
P.O. Box 1017, Maricopa, Arizona 85139
www.XPpublishing.com

ISBN: 978-1-621660-06-4

Printed in the United States of America for Worldwide Distribution

STEP Into DESTINY

FIND & FULFILL
YOUR GOD-GIVEN PURPOSE

DANIEL HYUN PARK

So many people ask me, "How can I know for sure what I was created to be and called to do?" Many share that they are floundering and feeling lost, without purpose or direction. Daniel Park addresses these very issues in his book, *Step Into Destiny*. He skillfully calls the reader to follow God's leading into fulfilled purpose. You will enjoy this book ... and if you have felt lost or confused in your journey, *Step Into Destiny* will help you discover a solid place to stand and clear vision for the future.

PATRICIA KING
XPMEDIA.COM

A perfect blend of practicality and depth, *Step Into Destiny* gives applicable insight to finding your destiny. Without hesitation or reservation, I recommend this work by Daniel Park. Seasoned believers and spiritual newborns, alike, can greatly benefit from reading this to-the-point and balanced message. The truths within this book will most certainly help you to discover and refine the path to your divinely ordered destiny.

DAVID DIGA HERNANDEZ
International Healing Evangelist
DavidHernandezMinistries.com

There is nothing more important in life than the discovery of one's divine purpose and destiny. In this timely book, Daniel Park does a masterful job of giving you the blueprint to success. You will discover exactly why you have been placed on earth.

TOURE ROBERTS
Executive Director
Artist Resource Center, One Church International
North Hollywood, California
onechurchla.org

Dedicated to

my pastors, Ryan & Joanne Lee

&

my church family at

Blessed International Fellowship

Acknowledgements

Holy Spirit, You gave me the blueprints for *Step Into Destiny* in three days and helped me every inch of the way. I couldn't do this without You. Please encounter those who read this book.

Dr. Myles E. Munroe, I'm so grateful that you invested your highly demanded time to add your extraordinary wisdom and excellent character to this book. God has used you to transform the face of the Church into a kingdom-minded people. Your impact on my life cannot be put into words. Thank you for not just believing in this book, but you also believe in me. You bring out the best in all of us. I'm so honored to be a spiritual son who will run with the vision to see His kingdom manifested on this earth.

Patricia King, you are such a trailblazer and an amazing spiritual mom to my generation. Thank you for believing in me, loving me, and helping to make my publishing dreams a reality. By the way, thanks for this cool title!

A big THANK YOU to seasoned intercessor, **Baerbel Neumann**. I'm grateful for your love and prayers for this book. After reading my first book, you prophesied that many more books would come. After hearing me preach the message "Thrive in Your Training Camp," you greatly encouraged me to put it into print. Well, here it is! Great rewards await you for your many years of faithfulness to the Lord. The best is still ahead. May you see the great revival you've been promised!

Special thanks to **Michelle Burkett** and the XP Publishing team for helping me to get this burning message out there!

Contents

Foreword

by

DR. MYLES E. MUNROE

This timely, erudite, eloquent, and immensely thought-provoking work gets to the heart of the deepest passions and aspirations of the human heart: to discover the path to personal purpose and meaning in life.

This is indispensable reading for those who want to understand their own potential to achieve greatness and live above the norm. This profound, heart-searching work – which spans the wisdom of the ages and yet breaks new ground in its approach – will possibly become a classic in this and the next generation.

This exceptional work by Daniel Park is one of the most profound, practical, principle-centered approaches to the subject of "purpose" that I have read in a long time. The author's approach to this timely issue brings a fresh breath of air that captivates the heart, engages the mind, and inspires the spirit of the reader.

The author's ability to leap over complicated theological and metaphysical jargon and reduce complex theories to simple, practical principles, which the least among us can understand, is amazing.

This work will challenge the intellectual and embrace the layman as it dismantles the mysterious soul search of mankind and delivers the profound in simplicity.

Daniel's approach awakens the untapped inhibiters that retard our personal development, and his antidotes empower us to rise above these self-defeating, self-limiting factors to a life of exploits in spiritual and mental advancement.

The author also integrates time-tested precepts into each chapter, giving each principle a practical application to life and making the entire process people-friendly.

Every sentence of *Step Into Destiny* is pregnant with wisdom, and I enjoyed the mind-expanding experience. I admonish you to plunge into this ocean of knowledge, and watch your life change for the better as you discover and manifest your life's purpose in your generation.

DR. MYLES E. MUNROE
Bahamas Faith Ministries International
International Third World Leader Association (ITWLA)
Nassau, Bahamas

Preface

Feeling lost? If you feel lost, you probably are.

Feeling unfulfilled? If so, it could be for good reason. I don't mean to offend anyone by being so direct. But the feelings of being lost and unfulfilled are serious symptoms of a greater problem, a problem that needs to be confronted. This book is not condemning but it *is* confrontational. Condemnation leaves us feeling hopeless, but confrontation from the Holy Spirit has the power to transform our lives! Confrontation is not always comfortable, but it *is* vital to see change. Get ready to be changed into a person who is no longer lost and unfulfilled, but who lives every day with purpose, passion, and precision!

FEEL LOST?

You don't have to feel lost. You don't have to be oblivious when it comes to what you should be doing with your life – future and present. You don't have to be clueless when it comes to these important questions:

- What is my God-given destiny?
- What should I do today so I can fulfill my destiny?

- What is God asking me to pour my life into during this season of my life?

All of these questions must be answered, and I trust that you will get satisfying answers from the Holy Spirit as you travel through this book.

While this book will help you to discover your destiny, that's not good enough. It's one thing to get pregnant, but unless you successfully carry the baby and give birth, the child will not be born into the world. Just being impregnated with your God-given vision is not enough. Out of the percentage of Christians who have accurately identified what God has called them to do, a much smaller percentage actually live it out successfully. Too many of God's people go to their grave with their mission unaccomplished, their hopes deferred, and their dreams unfulfilled. Their destiny remains a fantasy.

This is not OK.

Why does it happen?

Although they received a clear picture of their destiny, they chose to burn the very bridges that God set before them – those bridges cross over into their destiny. What are those "destiny bridges" that often get burned rather than crossed? We will talk about them in detail in this book.

Let me just say that if you despise the stepping stones to your destiny that God has laid before you, those stepping stones will become tombstones. But if you honor those stepping stones, they will become your milestones! This book will help you in more ways than just resonating with your God-given destiny; you will also learn how to practically walk it out and fulfill it, turning your stepping stones into milestones.

WHAT NOW?

Maybe you have already received an unforgettable glimpse of your God-designed destiny but your problem is "I don't know where to start?" Perhaps you've already identified your spiritual gifts, natural talents, inner passions, and life calling but you are confused as to what you should be doing with them at the moment. Doors seem closed. Opportunities minimal. And now the vision that God gave you for your life seems to be growing dim. You are frustrated.

What now?

Maybe you're a Christian who only has a general idea of what God wants you to do (such as love Him, glorify Him, take dominion, etc.) but you have no idea of the specific things that God has placed you on earth to do.

What now?

Or maybe you are privileged to know for certain the specific callings or divine assignments on your life but you have failed to co-operate with the Holy Spirit en route to your destiny. So you wonder why you haven't tasted the milk and honey from your Promised Land.

What now?

Perhaps you have learned enough to realize that you are part of the Body of Christ but you have no idea exactly where you fit. Maybe you're an arm that is trying to act like a leg, or an eye that is trying to act like the foot. Like misplaced pieces of a puzzle you are lost. (If you think about it, when one piece of the puzzle is out of order it has a nasty ripple effect.)

What now?

Or perhaps you do have a strong sense of what specific role you are to play in the Body of Christ but you have no idea how to be promoted into your proper place. Instead, you ignorantly demote yourself right out of your destiny by refusing to grow up, change, submit to God and others, and truly humble yourself.

Maybe you are one of those Christians drowning in false humility and assuming you don't have much to offer. As a result of that kind of God-insulting thinking, you have become a horrible steward of your time, talent, and destiny. Or it could be that you are on the other side of the spectrum. You really believe you have *much* to offer but you don't know that greatness in the kingdom of God is only gained through faithfulness and servanthood. You want to be an overnight success story, a shooting star ... but that's not how the kingdom of God operates – it's not *American Idol*.

If you want to be instantly transported to your destination and skip the journey God has planned for you, sadly, you will miss out on both the journey and the destiny.

Maybe you have an "others-dependent" mindset – you always try to get other people to do what only God can do for you. You look to powerful, influential, and wealthy people as your source instead of God; it is no wonder that God's destiny isn't happening for you.

Or perhaps your problem is an "overly-independent" mindset. Your ambition is to be a self-made man/woman. You are a lone ranger who doesn't know how to appreciate relationships, connections, friendships, mentorships, spiritual fathers and mothers. This mindset is an enemy of destiny, because God wants to use people to bless your life; He sends divine connections to connect you to your destiny.

If you can relate to any of these scenarios, then this book is for you.

FEEL UNFULFILLED?

You don't need to have lack of fulfillment eat away at your heart like termites. You don't have to waste your potential. You don't have to live just counting the years instead of making them count for time and eternity!

If you feel unfulfilled, there is probably *something* more and/or *something* else that God has called you to do, but you haven't been able to walk into it because you've been holding onto something you should have let go of, or you might have let go of something you should have held onto.

I don't know what those "somethings" are for you but the Holy Spirit does, and He's more than willing to bring clarity. Let me warn you: our God can be very blunt with us when we are missing His best for our lives.

None of us have any more time to waste. It's time we get out of Lost Land and Unfulfilled City and get back onto God's track for our lives. We need to get in step with the Holy Spirit – our Destiny Coach.

You might be thinking, "As far as I know, I'm on the right track!" But are you moving at the right speed? Are you running ahead of God or do you refuse to budge at His nudge? The Scriptures teach us to "Be not like a horse or a mule" (Psalm 32:9). The horse tends to be too wild and the mule tends to be too lazy, but we are called to walk in accordance with the Holy Spirit.

There is only one solution to this problem of feeling lost and unfulfilled, and apart from this solution our destiny will stay out of reach. We must learn to be led by the Holy Spirit, which includes being willing and able to follow His lead. Only then can we be at the right place at the right time, doing the right thing with the right team of people, never lost again and living a fulfilling life!

Our Lord Jesus never felt lost. He lived in step with the Holy Spirit and walked into all God had prepared for Him. He lived every day with purpose, passion, and precision.

- **Purpose:** For this purpose I was born and for this purpose I have come into the world – to bear witness to the truth. Everyone who is of the truth listens to my voice (John 18:37).

  The thief comes only to steal and kill and destroy. I came that they may have life and have it abundantly (John 10:10).

- **Passion:** His disciples remembered that it was written (about Jesus), "Zeal for your house will consume me" (John 2:17).

- **Precision:** Truly, truly, I say to you, the Son can do nothing of his own accord, but only what he sees the Father doing. For whatever the Father does, that the Son does likewise (John 5:19).

  Simon and his companions went to look for him, and when they found him, they exclaimed: "Everyone is looking for you!" Jesus replied, "Let us go somewhere else – to the nearby villages – so I can preach there also. That is why I have come" (Mark 1:36-38 NIV).

Jesus is our matchless model. As you venture through this book with a humble heart, you will begin to live with a strong sense of purpose, holy passion will overtake you, and you will live precisely in alignment with God's perfect will. As God speaks to you, you will learn how to maximize every season of your life and never get lost again!

CHAPTER ONE

What Is Destiny?

DESIGN OR DISCOVER?

I did not design the cover of this book. I'm a very limited artist so I was grateful to find someone with a whole lot more knowledge, skill, and experience to take on that task. When it comes to your destiny, you don't have to design it – this should cause a sigh of relief. Our God, who is perfect in knowledge, skill, and experience, has taken on this responsibility. Therefore, your responsibility is to simply discover your destiny and follow the Holy Spirit into it.

The same God who is behind the extravagant beauty of nature has handcrafted a destiny for you. Trust me, it's a whole lot bigger and better than you could ever imagine. "Now to him who is able to do far more abundantly than all that we ask or think, according to the power at work within us" (Ephesians 3:20). His destiny for us is so big that, apart from His ability, we will never be able to walk it out.

The Scriptures say, "We are his workmanship, created in Christ Jesus for good works, which God prepared beforehand, that we should walk in them" (Ephesians 2:10). Those "good works" that God "prepared beforehand" for you to walk in, culminate in your divine destiny. As you can see, God has already prepared it as a master chef would prepare a banqueting table of gourmet foods and scrumptious delicacies. Your job is to eat it – one bite at a time.

King David also wrote along these lines saying, "Your eyes saw my unformed substance; in your book were written, every one of them, the days that were formed for me, when as yet there was none of them" (Psalm 139:16). Long before David's first birthday, God had already destined that David would be anointed by Samuel, kill Goliath, be king, etc. God has a destiny book for you and me as well.

Aren't you glad that you don't have to determine your own destiny – only discover it? All-wise God has fashioned our destiny for us! That's comforting yet exhilarating to know, isn't it?

Now, just in case you are worried that God has maliciously planned a horrible destiny for you, let this Scripture expel that needless paranoia: "For I know the plans I have for you, declares the LORD, plans for welfare and not for evil, to give you a future and a hope" (Jeremiah 29:11). God's destiny for you is one of welfare (not to put you on welfare, but to prosper your life). It's something to look forward to!

Adam and Eve blew their future (through sin) when Satan got them to believe that God was keeping a great future away from them (see Genesis 3:5-6). Contrary to Satan's suggestions, God isn't keeping the most fulfilling destiny *from* you, but *for* you. To believe this truth will determine the quality of your future.

WANT A PREVIEW?

Do you know that God is more than willing to show you a preview of what exactly those "good works ... prepared beforehand" are? Do you know that He desires to give you a sneak peak into that "destiny book" David wrote about?

It happened to me at the age of fourteen. I knew God had saved me for a purpose so I kept bugging Him day and night about what that specific purpose was. I needed to know what He wanted me to do with my life! I told Him that I'd do whatever He would make clear to me.

Do you have that kind of resolution in your heart? Are you willing to boldly ask God to reveal His destiny for you? Are you also willing to do what He says? If so, get ready!

One morning, I awoke from a God encounter in my sleep. I was speaking almost uncontrollably in tongues and buzzing under the power of God. In a vivid dream, I had seen myself preaching to a crowd of young people and shouting "Hallelujah!" By the time I said "Hallelujah" the third time, the fire of the Holy Spirit torched the entire crowd! I saw young people dramatically repent of their sins, weep under the deep conviction of God's love, and tremble under the power of God. I even saw some of the young people vomiting (which I came to understand spoke of deliverance from evil spirits).

All I can tell you is that when I awoke from that most unforgettable dream, I knew in my heart of hearts what God had put me on this earth to do – it was to preach and welcome the Holy Spirit to do what only He can do! In the last fourteen years of my preaching ministry, I've preached in many meetings where I felt like I was literally having déjà vu, because what I saw in that significant dream kept happening over and over again in real life, in real time!

It's not easy to articulate the deep fulfillment you experience after you skim through some of the pages of your destiny book, and then you begin to see those pages come to pass before your very eyes! This is available to all of us. Jesus promised that the Holy Spirit would show us "the things that are to come" in our lives (John 16:13). Ask for it. Expect it. Experience it.

Jesus Knew It, Spoke It & Lived It

Jesus knew His destiny and He wasn't afraid to speak about His God-given assignment. He boldly declared in a public square:

> The Spirit of the Lord is upon me, because he has anointed me to proclaim good news to the poor. He has sent me to proclaim liberty to the captives and recovering of sight to the blind, to set at liberty those who are oppressed, to proclaim the year of the Lord's favor.
>
> —Luke 4:18-19

Jesus had this "destiny download" before He ever walked it out. Remember, this episode took place before He preached a single message, performed a single miracle, or did any kind of healing. Jesus knew His destiny, spoke it out, and then lived it. As He did, He found great fulfillment. He told His disciples, "My food is to do the will of him who sent me and to accomplish his work" (John 4:34). Just like food is satisfying to our bodies, there is a special satisfaction that comes to our souls when we know that we are living out God's specific will for our lives! Discover your destiny, declare it in faith, and then live it in love. That's fulfilling!

DON'T BE AFRAID OF HATERS

When insecure people hear you talk about your destiny, they can choke on your dream and then throw up on you. But there is no need to fear haters, because they cannot stop God's purposes for you. They didn't give you your destiny, and they can't take it away.

Joseph's brothers hated him because of his dreams; they threw him into a pit and eventually sold him into slavery in Egypt. What's ironic is that if Joseph's brothers had not sold him for twenty pieces of silver, Joseph would not have been positioned in Egypt to lead the world, which was the fulfillment of his destiny dream!

It was Jesus' claims about Himself and His destiny that attracted haters, like a bright light draws moths. When He spoke about His destiny, it drove the haters crazy, causing them to pin Jesus to an old rugged cross! Little did they know that they were setting Him up to *fulfill* His destiny, which was to die for the sins of the world and be raised from the dead on the third day!

When you get a download of your destiny and begin to see yourself as God sees you, and when you speak about your destiny from God's point of view and then actually start living it, haters will be drawn to you like sharks to fresh blood. There is no need to fear; their rejection of you can't abort your God-given destiny, but it can further propel you into it. You never know, you might be one hater away from your destiny.

FIND YOURSELF IN THE WORD

The declaration of destiny that Jesus made in Luke 4:17-19 was really something He had discovered in Isaiah 61:1-2. This is significant, because if what you believe to be your destiny is in contradiction to God's written Word, you are in error; it's not from God. If you can't find scriptural support for what you believe God has called you to do, you might have caught Satan's vision for your life, not God's.

For God's people, the Word of God must be the strongest supporter of your destiny. If you know what God has called you to do, get all the Scriptures that support your calling into your heart! Your destiny must be linked to the Word. You can't separate your destiny from God's Word; they must function in unity. The Word of God is your destiny's umbilical cord.

The Word of God is your destiny's umbilical cord.

Which Bible characters cause your heart to do backflips? Thank God for all the characters in the Bible, especially those who successfully lived out their destinies, and specifically those who speak to us about our own destinies.

Yes, we believe and embrace the whole Bible, but what are some of your *favorite* verses in the Scriptures? If you had to pick life-verses, which would they be?

One life-verse of Aimee Semple McPherson (1880-1944) was, "Jesus Christ is the same yesterday and today and forever" (Hebrews 13:8). She knew it was her destiny to raise up a people who would believe that the same Jesus who healed two-thousand years ago was still actively healing the sick today through His church! She saw many dramatic healings and undeniable miracles as she ministered to the sick all over the country. She became the founder of the International Church of the Foursquare, which has 60,000 churches in 144 countries. Many of those churches have Hebrews 13:8 inscribed on their sanctuary walls, and many healing miracles continue to happen through their denomination. McPherson did not just firmly believe Hebrews 13:8 but imparted the revelation of it to countless millions around the world.

You are destined for more than just living out your life-verses; you are also to impart the revelation of them! You aren't on earth to just take up space – you are here to communicate. If you are faithful to communicate what God has destined you to convey, your life-sermons will outlive you.

FIND YOUR LIFE-SERMON

What are your life-sermons? What has God put you on this earth to specifically communicate to the people He desperately loves? God will take your favorite life-verses that He has fire-branded upon your heart and add your unduplicatable testimony, causing them to work together like gunpowder and fire. When your life-verses and your life-story conjoin and combust, you have a life-sermon. The following questions will help you identify your life-sermons:

- If you could write one sentence on a highly visible billboard, what would it read?

- If you can dictate one sentence that will remain on your tomb-stone, what would it preach?

- If you could write a book on only one topic, what would it be?

- If someone would write your biography twenty years after you pass away, what would the title be?

The world needs your message, and you must be the voice God has called you to be! You don't need to be a preacher to have a life-sermon; you just need to have a close walk with God and an understanding of your destiny. You also need to be grounded in the Word of God, because your life-sermon will be rooted in Scripture.

GOD IS THE POET, YOU ARE THE POEM

The Bible tells us, "For we are his workmanship, created in Christ Jesus for good works, which God prepared beforehand, that we should walk in them" (Ephesians 2:10).

That verse is so packed with meaning! What does it mean to be the workmanship of God? The Greek word for workmanship is *poiema,* from which we get our word *poem.* God is a Poet and you are His poem. If you speak negatively about God's poem or think that it's not worth being heard, that's an insult to our Poet God.

When God fashioned you into a new creation in Christ, He destined for you to communicate a message. Poems communicate, don't they? Poems usually contain a number of messages but seem to have main points or common threads. As each stanza of a poem can carry a unique message, each season of your life can (and will) have a timely message.

What are the main points or common threads that weave through the poem of your life? You don't need to be shy, because your life-sermons are not really about you; they are God's poems through which He reveals Himself – you and I are just props. As we serve as His props, we fulfill our destiny – our destiny is not using God, but being used by Him to reveal Himself! For His pleasure and glory, we exist (see Colossians 1:16).

HE DOESN'T CAUSE THE HARM; HE REDEEMS!

Do you know that God's grace will even take all your past mistakes and hurts and morph them into life-changing messages?

The Scriptures promise us, "For those who love God all things work together for good, for those who are called according to his purpose" (Romans 8:28). God is such a skilled Poet with endless creativity that He is going to use all the raw material of your life experiences to create a masterpiece. Now, please don't say it was God that made you sin! Nor was it God who caused you to go through your bitter rejections and traumas. God is not the author of evil!

> Let no one say when he is tempted, "I am being tempted by God," for God cannot be tempted with evil, and he himself tempts no one. But each person is tempted when he is lured and enticed by his own desire.
>
> —James 1:13-14

The authors of our scars and mistakes are the sin factor, our stupidity, and the selfish lusts of humanity – not God. But God is the Great Redeemer who can and will recycle all the garbage of our past experiences and make something useful and beautiful out of it! He will include your testimony in His poem.

Did you ever wonder how the Israelites got the weapons that they warred with while they were in the wilderness? After the Israelites checked out of Egypt, they fought a number of major wars. But given the fact that they were slaves for four hundred years and left Egypt abruptly, where did they get their weapons?

Remember when Pharaoh's armies came after the Israelites while they were crossing the Red Sea, and the sea closed in on the Egyptians (see Exodus 14)? The Jewish historian, Josephus, records that after the waters crushed the Egyptians, their mighty weapons were washed ashore, and the Israelites were able to pick them up and use them.

Did you catch the irony?

What the enemy used to try to destroy Israel – Israel was able to use to destroy their enemies! I'm convinced that the Israelites used those same weapons to eventually take their Promised Land (or destiny).

What weapons did Satan form against you? How did Satan attack you? Do you know that the very weapons Satan formed against you can now be used to destroy him and his kingdom? As you do so, you are fulfilling destiny.

So don't be afraid of sharing your testimony; it can be the very key that will unlock someone else's faith to overcome as you did. Your testimony might be the very weapon that gets you into your Promised Land.

THE WORLD NEEDS YOUR MESSAGE

Harmony Dust lost her virginity at the age of fourteen. As a young girl, she was no stranger to rape and abuse. The boyfriend she was supporting – and dying to keep – continually cheated on her and tore her heart apart. She became a stripper for three years to pay off her debts and support that man she was addicted to. She felt shameful and worthless. This was all Satan's perfect plan for Harmony.

But God stepped in.

He became the Father she never had but always wanted and desperately needed. He showed her love in its truest and purest form. He healed her of her many deep scars. Harmony now leads a dynamic ministry called *Treasures*. She and her team, which consists of women who were even more broken than her, are on a mission to help women in the sex industry. They lead hurting women into the healing love

> **The very weapons Satan formed against you can now be used to destroy him and his kingdom!**

of Jesus and a life of divine purpose. The world needs Harmony's message, and she's not afraid to shout it from the rooftops! Her life-Scriptures and life-story have merged together to form a world-changing sermon! With her life-sermons, she's fulfilling destiny.

The world also needs your message. Have you located your life-sermons? Are you writing yourself off and hiding God's poem, or are you stepping out in faith as God opens doors and His Spirit leads? You aren't on earth to take up space; you are here to communicate! Death and life are in the power of your tongue (Proverbs 18:21). We will leave this world, but our words will remain.

Don't Say, "I Don't Have Much!"

I hope you can see that you have a lot to offer this world. Remember, the world is in its dysfunctional state, not because Jesus didn't do His job, but because we haven't fulfilled our destinies. For your own sake and this lost world, don't bury your destiny by saying, "I don't have much!"

Jesus told an unforgettable story of a master who gave three servants talents according to their abilities (see Matthew 25:14-30). One received five talents, another received two, and the third received one talent. The servant who received five talents immediately used what he was given and made five more. The servant who received two talents was also a good steward of what he was given and doubled it. But the servant with one talent buried it. He didn't use what he was given but, instead, he hid it away. When the master came to check on them, he was pleased with the faithfulness of the first two servants but furious at the last servant!

Why didn't the servant with one talent do anything with what he was given? Could it be that he compared himself to the other servants and thought, "My calling isn't as impressive as theirs; I might as well just do nothing?" Even today, there are Christians who compare themselves with others and despise their own destiny, which includes their gifts, calling, and responsibilities. According to this parable, that is extremely unwise.

The master rewarded the two servants, who were faithful to use what they were given, with greater responsibilities. He told them, "Well done, good and faithful slave. You were faithful with a few things, I will put you in charge of many things; enter into the joy of your master" (Matthew 25:23 NASB).

But they were given more than just increased responsibilities; they were also given the master's joy! There is a divine joy that we experience when we have been productive with what the Lord has given to us! When you are fulfilling your destiny, you feel the pleasure of God.

If you are not a good steward of your time, gifts, and calling, you will feel the lack of joy. If you idolize or criticize those who are living their destinies, all while neglecting your own, you will be unfulfilled.

By the way, one talent actually came to sixteen years of salary ($700,000 in the U.S.). That was more than enough money to do something significant! Just as the master gave all three servants everything they needed for their success, God, too, has given you an amazing destiny and everything you need to be successful in your God-given assignment! Don't bury your destiny – maximize it.

DESTINY QUESTIONS

1. Has God given you a snapshot of your destiny? What have you seen so far?

   both in evangelism as
   e wuts. "a sea of creativity"

2. What are your life-sermons? Remember, it's the fusion of your favorite Scriptures and your life-story.

   1, "Create in me a clean heart
   They that wait upon the LORD...",
   he Kingdom of God".
   t up — Holy and Righteous Living.

3. What are some of the most difficult challenges that you have faced in your life? Has a powerful message been birthed through those challenges?

CHAPTER TWO

Discover Your Destiny

I f you really want deep understanding of a poem, spend much time with the poet and ask him questions. If you really want to understand a book, get to know its author on a personal level. To discover your destiny, get to know its Designer, hang out with Him often, and inquire of Him. Since God has already penned your destiny, He will tell you about it as you get to know Him. When you hang out with people, they talk about what's on their hearts. Your future is on God's heart, and as you spend time with Him and get to know His heart, you find your destiny. His thoughts about your destiny are too many to count; they are as numerous as the sand of the seas (see Psalm 139:17-18).

1. Get to Know the Author

The following verse assures us that God has an amazing destiny for us:

> For I know the plans I have for you, declares the LORD, plans for welfare and not for evil, to give you a future and a hope.
>
> —Jeremiah 29:11

While this is a famous verse that's often quoted in sermons, posters, and postcards, it's not often presented along with the two verses that come next. While Jeremiah 29:11 conveys to us that we have a destiny, the next two verses give us the roadmap to discover that destiny:

> Then you will call upon me and come and pray to me, and I will hear you. You will seek me and find me, when you seek me with all your heart.
>
> —Jeremiah 29:12-13

Are you seeing it? If you want to know your destiny, you need to pray and seek after God wholeheartedly – get to know Him. You might be thinking, "I need to get to know my destiny, not Him!" Well, that attitude reveals that your destiny is your idol.

If all your hopes and dreams are fulfilled but you don't have intimacy with God, that's emptiness!

If you only want to know your destiny but skip intimacy with God, you aren't ready for your destiny. It's only through our intimacy with God that true fruitfulness comes (see John 15:4). If you get to truly know God and become familiar with His voice, discovering and fulfilling your destiny will be an easy by-product. But if you only want to know your destiny, you will miss both God and your destiny.

Only as we enjoy intimacy with God can we actually exude His heart of love (see 1 John 4:8). And we will only receive eternal rewards for what was done in God's love (see 1 Corinthians 13:1-3). While I'm on earth, I want to successfully live out my destiny and then be eternally rewarded for my work, don't you? This can only happen when we live out our destiny from intimacy with God.

HEAR FROM GOD FOR YOURSELF

Yes, prophetic words from credible others can help confirm your God-given destiny, but you must also hear from God for yourself! Why? Discovering your destiny from another person's prophetic words doesn't require personal intimacy with God! Those who depend on prophetic words to discover their destiny – instead of seeking God and hearing directly from Him – are setting themselves up for trouble. They will jump from meeting to meeting in an attempt to get another prophetic word, trying to figure out what to do next with their lives. Their phone bills will get ridiculously high, because they constantly phone their favorite prophet. Sadly, even with all the prophetic words they've gathered, they will still be lost. But what more can you expect from someone who has settled for a second-hand relationship with the Lord?

Only God has the right to tell you what your destiny is, because He's the One who created you. I can wrongly prophesy to an iPod and say that its destiny is to be used as high-class toilet paper. Yet, I don't get to vote – I'm not the manufacturer. Steve Job and Apple already determined the destiny of the iPod. Instead of trying to compile a thousand opinions about your destiny, spend time getting to know your Manufacturer; no one knows you like He does.

The Scriptures tell us that "The people who know their God shall *stand firm* and *take action*" (Daniel 11:32). As you get to know the Author of your destiny, you will find the strength to "stand firm" in what God has called you to do, rather than hopping like a fickle frog from one thing to another. Be a personal friend of God. Hear from Him on a regular basis so that when you do "take action" toward your destiny, you will be on track with His plan for your life.

By the way, you can't know God personally without being compelled to take action. Laziness is a symptom of people not knowing God for themselves. As we intimately know Him and inquire of Him, the Holy Spirit will continually give us wisdom in regard to specific actions to take.

The psalmist wrote, "Delight yourself in the LORD, and he will give you the desires of your heart" (Psalm 37:4). As knowing Him becomes your delight, He will download His desires and dreams for your life into your heart and He will partner with you to bring them to pass!

2. Ask Him

This might sound overly simplistic but if you really want to know your destiny, ask God. It doesn't hurt to ask and it helps a whole lot!

The Scriptures strongly admonish that "If any of you lacks wisdom, let him ask God, who gives generously to all without reproach, and it will be given him. But let him ask in faith, with no doubting, for the one who doubts is like a wave of the sea that is driven and tossed by the wind. For that person must not suppose that he will receive anything from the Lord" (James 1:5-7).

As a young Christian, I had a much clearer understanding of my destiny than most people I knew. It was not a coincidence that

I also bugged God about revealing my destiny more often than any-one I knew. When you ask God for wisdom about your destiny, ex-pect nothing less than clear answers! We need to ask confidently and expectantly. We have not, because we ask not (James 4:2).

Why You Need to Know This Stuff

I'm not implying that God will show you every detail of your life in advance (1 Corinthians 13:9 says that "we know in part") but I'm convinced that He will show you some encouraging and useful stuff as you ask Him.

Why is it so important to know what God has for you one, three, five, ten, thirty, fifty years down the line? Shouldn't we just take it one day at a time? Yes, we are to give our best today and not stress about tomorrow, but we can also live with the advantage of knowing our fu-ture.

God gave Abraham a blueprint of his amazing destiny, and those blue-prints helped Abraham to not give up when times got tough.

Joseph also had a snapshot of his destiny. I'm sure that when he was be-ing sold as a slave and thrown in the dungeon, the prophetic vision he had received from God helped keep his hopes alive! I believe that Jo-seph thought to himself, "God's not through with me yet! As I hold onto Him, and He to me, the dream will still come to pass!" Aston-ishingly, we never see Joseph complaining or negative at the lowest points of his life. It's because He knew God and God's plan for his life!

> When you ask God for wisdom about your destiny, expect nothing less than clear answers!

Another reason it is to your advantage to find out what God has prepared for you is that you can start preparing for the future! Ever since he was a young lad, David knew he would be king. I'm sure that as he was interning in King Saul's palace, he was actively taking notes and preparing himself to lead the nation.

When Jesus was a young boy, He knew that He was called for His Father's business (Luke 2:49) and He prepared Himself by studying the Scriptures and picking the brains of the best Bible teachers in Israel.

Since Joseph was able to supernaturally perceive that famine was coming, he got the whole nation of Egypt ready for it; thus, Egypt actually succeeded in famine instead of dying in it. It was because Joseph discerned what was going to happen in the future that he knew what he needed to do in his today, which was to store up a bunch of food during the time of plenty. Honestly, too many people waste their "today" because they don't know what God desires to do in their tomorrows. "Where there is no prophetic vision the people cast off restraint" (Proverbs 29:18).

When I was fourteen years old, I knew God had called me to preach so I spent much time preparing myself for this great destiny. After I knew what God called me to do in my future, I never wasted my time with video games, and I learned to turn off the television. Instead, I got my face in the Word of God and wrote down all the insights I received from the Holy Spirit. There were long stretches of time when nobody asked me to preach or teach. I eventually took the insights Holy Spirit shared with me and began to share them by writing an Internet blog where I posted hundreds of un-preached sermons. When doors began to open for me to preach, I now had a large pool of revelation to pull from. My years of faithful blogging also prepared me to write books, which is another facet of my God-given destiny.

MAXIMIZE YOUR SEASONS

Through creation, God has taught us the importance of seasons. In nature, there is a season for sowing and another season for reaping. If you try to harvest during winter, you aren't going to be very fruitful. All year round, productive farmers know what they must do during each season. If we want to get the max out of our destinies, we need to understand what season we are in and what we are to do in that season.

God wants us to maximize the seasons of our lives instead of getting bitter about them. Those who are bitter about not seeing their big dreams immediately fulfilled are wasting their time and emotions! They really need to locate who, where, and how God wants them to serve *right now,* and maximize their seasons! When you maximize your seasons, you maximize your destiny!

When Paul was in prison, he knew it was the season to write. Those letters that Paul penned from prison are in your Bible today being read all over the world! As a discerning man, he didn't get bitter, complain, or waste his time; he made the most out of every season. The Scriptures tell us, "For everything there is a season, and a time for every matter under heaven" (Ecclesiastes 3:1).

When we talk about maximizing seasons, we are not referring to the four seasons of each year. Your seasons might be much longer or shorter than three months. Seasons speak of a strategic period of time in which God gives you unique opportunities. The *Unger Bible Dictionary* defines a season as "a space of time for opportunity." In every season of your life, you have the opportunity to progress or digress toward your destiny. In every season, there are epic opportunities to mature, change, receive, give, serve, etc. Never get discouraged during any of your seasons; discern the opportunity that God has placed before you and maximize each season of your life.

INVESTING OR WASTING TIME?

Since I saw what God had in store for me in my future, I was also able to see what I should and shouldn't spend time doing in the present. Some people are described as "the jack of all trades but the master of none." These people have many interests and pursuits, but they never become an expert at any of them. They have many projects going on, but never complete any of them. They have lots of ambitions, but don't accomplish anything. They have a second-grade education in everything, but a Ph.D. in nothing. They remain mediocre in many things and fail to leave their mark in the world. That is tragic! We are called to be masters of our gifts, callings, and destinies!

> We are called to dominate time, make it our servant, and maximize it.

One thing God specifically showed me was that my destiny didn't include being a musician. He spoke to me about not wasting my time trying to be a musician. But He promised that He would always surround me with musicians as I stayed true to my assignment. Therefore, I've not wasted my time trying to get better at twenty instruments. I want to master my calling from God instead of perfecting my hobbies. I'm not saying hobbies are always a waste of time, since they can help us relax and reconnect with family and friends, but if you are investing more time trying to perfect your hobbies than mastering your calling from God, you're lost – very lost.

We are commanded to, "Look carefully then how you walk, not as unwise but as wise, making the best use of the time, because the days are evil. Therefore do not be foolish, but understand what the will of the Lord is" (Ephesians 5:15-17).

Without wisdom from God about our future, we will devour our time instead of redeeming it. As a boxer will seek to beat their opponent to the point of unconsciousness and then throw the knockout punch, time will try to throw us into a confused tailspin and then defeat us with its final and fatal blow. We must not be mastered by time but, rather, master our time! God's original plan was that we would have dominion over the earth (Genesis 1:26), and time is not from heaven but from earth. We are called to dominate time, make it *our* servant, and maximize it. This can only happen when we know God's specific will for our lives, our seasons, and each day.

Is It OK to Boast About My Future?

Someone might argue that we shouldn't boast about all that we will do in the future, since the Bible teaches:

> Come now, you who say, "Today or tomorrow we will go into such and such a town and spend a year there and trade and make a profit"– yet you do not know what tomorrow will bring. What is your life? For you are a mist that appears for a little time and then vanishes. Instead you ought to say, "If the Lord wills, we will live and do this or that."
>
> —James 4:13-15

I agree that we shouldn't flippantly blurt out that we will one day do this and that, because James tells us instead we ought to be saying, "If the Lord wills, we will..." But does that mean we have to say, "If the Lord wills..." before we talk about anything future tense? You will drive people crazy.

Instead, we ought to walk closely with the Lord and clearly hear from Him about our destiny so that when we do talk about what the future has in store for us, we speak what God has revealed instead of stating arrogant assumptions that are independent of God's prophetic revelation and direction.

It's not wrong to talk about your exciting future or destiny, but it's wrong to blab things that aren't God's will. Be wise about those before whom you cast your pearls of prophetic destiny (Matthew 7:6). But, unless He specifically directs you otherwise, it's not illegal to share what God has shown you about your future – Jesus did.

How do you know what His will is for your life? Get to know Him, and ask Him questions with confident expectation that He will answer you in a way that's clear to you.

Do you love God? Then the Bible promises that God has amazing things in store for you (we can call those things: destiny)! But not just that, the Word of God promises us that by the Holy Spirit we can and will know what those amazing things are!

> No eye has seen, no ear has heard, no mind has conceived what God has prepared for those who love him, but God has revealed it to us by his Spirit.
>
> —1 Corinthians 2:9-10 NIV

This is a wonderful promise and privilege to claim in prayer and take full advantage of. Tell the Lord, "You promised to reveal my destiny to me by the Holy Spirit. I ask You for it and thank You in advance."

3. CHECK THE FULFILLMENT FACTOR

After you: (1) get to know the Author, and (2) ask Him, now (3) check the fulfillment factor. This is another valid key to discovering your destiny.

A microphone cannot be satisfied being used as a football. A laptop cannot be happy when it's used as a frying pan. A Starbucks cannot be thrilled about becoming a barn, full of animals.

When the microphone serves to amplify sound, it's fulfilled. When the laptop is used as a computer, it's happy. When Starbucks is serving coffee, it stays in great shape. When you live out your destiny, that's when you will be most fulfilled!

As an apostle, it was part of Paul's destiny to establish communities of love and bring the unity of the faith among believers. That is why he transparently wrote to the Philippi church, "Complete my joy by being of the same mind, having the same love, being in full accord and of one mind" (Philippians 2:2).

What completes your joy? With some of the youth I mentored, I would ask, "If you had ten million dollars to spend for a cause, how would you spend it?" I was trying to get them to discover what would bring them the most fulfillment, because that would help them to identify their destiny.

As a young man, Reinhardt Bonnke, a German evangelist who led over 52 million souls to Christ, received the call of God to "plunder hell and populate heaven." The Holy Spirit showed him heart-consuming visions of Africa washed in the blood of Jesus. As of this writing, he is 72 years old, and I heard him recently say that doing crusades in Africa is still "my holy addiction!" He explained how extremely difficult it was for him to stay away from doing crusades. Do you have a holy addiction?

What Is Your Holy Hatred?

The complimentary flip side to your fulfillment factor is your holy hatred. What problem in the world do you hate more than anything? Now, please don't say it's being in traffic, a bad hair day, or anything else that's superficial. Dig down deeper into your spirit, and locate that for which God has given you a holy indignation. The Scripture teaches us to "Be angry and do not sin" (Ephesians 4:26). There is such a thing as holy anger and it can actually help you locate your destiny.

It was seeing the Hebrews living as slaves that made Moses' blood boil. Sure enough, his divine hatred was directly connected to his destiny.

John G. Lake was one of sixteen children. He spent much of his childhood in hospitals, with doctors, and at funerals, because eight of his siblings died young from different sicknesses. As an adult, he had a brother who had been handicapped for twenty-two years and was bleeding to death; his sister had five cancerous tumors in her body; and his wife was plagued by tuberculosis and heart disease. Out of desperation, his family took his brother to a healing ministry in Illinois, and his brother was miraculously healed! Hope for healing began to fill John G. Lake's heart. He had not dreamed it was possible before. As he started studying the Word, he came to see that Jesus destroyed sickness because it was an oppression of the devil (see Acts 10:38). In his writing titled, "How I Came to Devote My Life to the Ministry of Healing," Lake explained how sickness became his holy hatred. When the sister who had the five tumors became unconscious, without a pulse, Lake journaled his reaction:

No words of mine can convey to another soul the … flame of hatred for death and sickness that the Spirit of God has stirred within me. The very wrath (of God) seemed to possess my soul![1]

Lake then rebuked the power of sickness and death in the name of Jesus, and his sister was raised from the dead and completely healed!

When the doctors told him that his dying wife was hopeless and as good as dead, that same fire started to burn within him. He laid his hands on her and prayed fervently. Instantly, she too was healed. This was the beginning of Lake's healing ministry that touched the world! He found and fulfilled his destiny.

What fans the fires of holy anger in you? What breaks your heart more than anything? Human trafficking? Ignorant Christians? Powerless Christianity? Poverty? Divorce? Abortion? Youth who are in Satan's grip? Addictions? Prodigal sons and daughters?

Once you discover your destiny, you will need to make sure your life is in order, because anything that is out of order cannot fulfill its original purpose.

---

[1] John G. Lake, "How I Came to Devote My Life to the Ministry of Healing" *Diary of God's General: Excerpts From the Miracle Ministry of John G. Lake* (Harrison House, Inc., March 2004), p. 55.

DESTINY QUESTIONS

1. **What are you doing to prepare yourself for your destiny?**

   Asking God about my identity. Trying to discover who I am, what ~~make~~ moves me, etc.

2. **What does God want you to specifically focus on in this season of your life?**

   Writing? I've been journalling alot lately. Even thinking about maybe writing more songs.

3. **Is there anything, which has nothing to do with your calling, that you waste too much of your time pursuing?** Still

   trying to figure this one out since I'm still unsure, but I pursue having more children and it seems to be a fruitless pursuit

4. **What completes your joy and stirs up holy hatred?**

   writing a revelutionary song has brought fulfilment in the past.
   Definately, the sex slave trade stirs up holy hatred! as does depression and divorce.

CHAPTER THREE

Life In Order

Jim Bakker was a very prominent minister who God called to pioneer Christian television. He and his wife, Tammy Faye, experienced unusual favor, as they were in step with the Holy Spirit and faithful to their assignment. They were used by God to establish the largest Christian television network of their time. However, things took a sour turn shortly after Jim took on the building of Heritage USA, which was a Christian resort and amusement park. He got so busy with the project that his family life began to crumble. This led to his highly publicized act of adultery. To make matters only worse, because the finances surrounding Heritage USA weren't handled properly, Jim had to serve almost five years in prison! He had a mental breakdown, went through a painful divorce, and was out of the ministry. His life was in disorder!

In his honest autobiographical book, *I Was Wrong*, Jim stated that although he was absolutely called by God to establish Christian television and even to establish a Christian retreat center, spending all that time and effort building a state-of-the-art Christian Disneyland was not an order from the Lord; rather, it was conceived by the seed of selfish ambition.

Looking back at all this, Jim wrote that while he sincerely thought he was doing a work for God, he was wrong to get sucked into the project like he did. He admits that his greed took him overboard. What started out as a God-ordained pet project turned into a fleshly Frankenstein monster. God even sent people to rebuke Jim for his insatiable obsession to build Heritage USA. James Robison sternly told him, "Jim, you are committing fornication with brick and mortar."[2] Yet, Jim wouldn't listen and only resented the corrective words. If he had stayed on the right track, only fighting the battles that God ordered him to fight, could he have avoided much of his turmoil? I believe so.

THE KING WHO BECAME A LEPER[3]

King Uzziah had just experienced God's mercy as God healed him of a terminal illness. However, even after this dramatic miracle, King Uzziah had an evil thought born in him. This wicked thought was, "I think I'd make a great priest!" You might be thinking, "What's wrong with wanting to be a priest?"

God had anointed Uzziah to be the king of Israel and to lead their armies. Uzziah was gifted and called to do just that. Yet King Uzziah coveted somebody else's calling and, hence, he got off of God's course for his life. He kept insisting to the priests that he would work the priestly duties of the tabernacle. They desperately warned him to stay in his lane and off theirs, explaining that it was dishonoring to the Lord.

[2] Jim Bakker, *I was Wrong*, (Thomas Nelson, October 1997), p. 467.
[3] See 2 Chronicles 26.

He refused.

Then, without coincidence, leprosy struck Uzziah. Leprosy is a skin disorder, which causes important parts of the body to eventually fall off or malfunction.

Under the Old Covenant, lepers were expelled from living among the people of God. They had to live in separate colonies and were despised as unclean. Uzziah went from being the most honored man in Israel to the most despised. He was no longer allowed into the house of God, which represented the presence of God. To sum it up: when he got off God's plan and purpose for his life, his life got out of order!

Biblically speaking, leprosy is often used as a picture of sin. When we try to fulfill another person's calling while despising our own, we open the door to sin. This happens partly because when we aren't doing what God called us to do, we feel empty inside and empty hearts crave anything – even junk.

When we covet another's calling while despising our own, we get struck with spiritual leprosy, which brings disorder into our lives. This disorder causes precious parts of the Body of Christ to malfunction. For example, if God has called you to be an eye in the Body of Christ but you insist on being a finger, you will function no better than an eye that's been plucked. You will be out of order.

The worst thing about being in rebellion toward God's will for our lives is that we will be missing out on the potential pleasure of His presence. It is when you are in the center of God's will for your life that you feel the pleasure and presence of God in a more concentrated way. The closer we dance with the Holy Spirit, the more of His presence we feel. If you want to do a solo dance performance and shove the Holy Spirit away, you will end up just being full of yourself.

Expensive, Wonderful & Out of Order

Recently, the Lord spoke to my heart saying, "My kingdom is a parking lot full of Mercedes, BMWs, and Ferraris that are out of order." I understood what He meant. When something is out of order, it doesn't matter how expensive or wonderful it is, because it will remain as wasted potential. Our lives are expensive. The shed blood of Jesus forever proved the value of each person. Yet many lives are still out of order.

God is in the business of making wonderful people with wonderful destinies. The psalmist couldn't help but declare, "I praise you, for I am fearfully and wonderfully made. Wonderful are your works; my soul knows it very well" (Psalm 139:14). This means that everyone ought to be absolutely blown away in sheer wonder when they observe our lives. However, that only happens when our lives are in order. The opposite of order is disarray, chaos, out of sync, out of place, broken, lost, and unfulfilled.

It's Not Enough to be Spirit-Filled

Those out of order BMWs and Ferraris can be full of gas but still be unable to function properly. Although gas is vital for a car to function, there needs to be more than a full tank of gas for the car to function in order.

We are vehicles of God's kingdom; our gasoline is the Holy Spirit. Zechariah prophesied, "Not by might nor by power, but by my Spirit, says the Lord Almighty" (Zechariah 4:6 NIV). Jesus stated, "You will receive power when the Holy Spirit comes on you" (Acts 1:8 NIV). Being Spirit-filled is a must if we are going to operate to our fullest potential. But there are some Christians who have been filled with the Spirit in the most dramatic way, yet their lives are still not in order.

On the day of Pentecost, the wind of the Holy Spirit was blowing and His gifts were in great manifestation, but that did not mean that their lives were automatically in order. Yes, it was an imperative first step, but it was not the automatic guarantee of order. The Corinthian church experienced the powerful infilling of the Holy Spirit and even moved in all the gifts of the Spirit, but their church was far from being in order.

Even when creation experienced the wind of the Holy Spirit, it did not automatically come into order. There was still disarray.

> The earth was without form and void, and darkness was over the face of the deep. And the Spirit of God was hovering over the face of the waters.
>
> —Genesis 1:2

The earth came into order only after God's voice was heard and obeyed!

> And God said, "Let there be light," and there was light. And God saw that the light was good ...
>
> —Genesis 1:3-4

It was only after creation came into order that God saw it was good.

After I experienced the powerful baptism of the Holy Spirit in the summer of 1997, my life was strongly impacted. It was an important step for my life, but my life was, honestly, still in disarray for a number of years. It was only after I learned to hear and obey the voice of God that my life started to get good – real good. Thank God for the infilling of the Holy Spirit, but we need to grow into people who also hear from God and are led by His Spirit.

ARE YOUR STEPS ORDERED BY GOD?

Simply put: Your life will only come into order when the Lord orders your steps. There is no way around this principle. "The steps of a good man are *ordered* by the LORD: and he (God) delights in his way" (Psalm 37:23 NKJV). God delights when we follow His orders. It's only when our steps are ordered by the Lord that we stop wasting potential. Since He is our Manufacturer, He loves to see His creation operating at his or her potential.

If your life is in complete disorder, it's not because God did a poor job when He created you; it's more probable that your steps haven't been ordered of Him. When He stepped right, you stepped left. When He stepped forward, you stepped back. When He said, "Stay," you said, "No." The result is disarray, chaos, being out of sync, out of place, broken, lost, and unfulfilled.

FROM PEOPLE OF PENTECOST TO PEOPLE OF THE PROPHETIC

We need to be more than people of Pentecost (who have experienced the infilling and movement of the Holy Spirit). We must become people of the prophetic (who hear and are led by the voice of the Holy Spirit).

When Jesus was baptized at the Jordan River, the power of the Holy Spirit came upon Him:

> As soon as Jesus was baptized, he went up out of the water. At that moment heaven was opened, and he saw the Spirit of God descending like a dove and lighting on him.
>
> —Matthew 3:16 NIV

Yet, Jesus was more than a Person of Pentecost; He was also a Person of the prophetic:

> Then Jesus was led by the Spirit into the desert to be tempted by the devil.
>
> —Matthew 4:1 NIV

A Life in Order Creates Order

Being filled and led by the Spirit were Jesus' secret keys to His successful life and ministry. There is no order when our steps aren't directed of the Lord.

Since Jesus' life was in order, everywhere He went He brought order to the chaos. He brought order where there was sickness and healing resulted. He brought order when there were natural disasters and peace resulted. He brought order when there was hunger and provision resulted. He brought order to hopelessness and condemnation, and changed lives were the result. He brought order to those who were demonized and deliverance resulted.

Do you see that it's only when our lives are in order that we can bring order to our world? Do you also understand that the only way to experience order in your life is to have your steps ordered of the Lord?

Aren't Good Motives Good Enough?

I remember as a baby Christian I had just experienced the infilling of the Holy Spirit. I prayed for hours at a time, lived full of holy zeal, and had supernatural compassion, but I wasn't a Spirit-led person. I was led by raw emotions, sometimes common sense, and often by the advice of others. But as children of God, it's our great privilege to be led by the Spirit of God Himself: "For all who are led by the Spirit of God are sons of God" (Romans 8:14). In fact, a life of God-led decisions ought to be our trademark as children of God. Yes, those who have been filled with the Holy Spirit will have a desire to be led by the Holy Spirit, but desiring something and living it are two separate things.

During that time, I had good motives but made bad choices. I remember often being physically sick because I would totally neglect my body while frantically delivering pizzas that God never ordered. I hope you get the idea.

Paul wanted to preach the gospel in Asia and Bithynia. I'm sure he had the right motivation, but it was the wrong plan. While having the right motive is important, so is having the right plan.

> And they went through the region of Phrygia and Galatia, *having been forbidden by the Holy Spirit* to speak the word in Asia. And when they had come up to Mysia, they attempted to go into Bithynia, but the Spirit of Jesus did not allow them.
>
> —Acts 16:6-7

Since Paul was tuned into the Holy Spirit, he wasn't going to be a fool with good motives. Paul knew that the consequences for getting out of God's will would have been devastating. You need the right plan and you need to be led by the Spirit of God.

Paul could have argued with the Holy Spirit and said, "Jesus gave the Great Commission to go into all the world and make disciples of all nations" (Matthew 28:19). He could have stubbornly gone to Asia and possibly died prematurely before completing His race. I'm sure Paul knew what Jesus said, but it was the Holy Spirit that gave Him the wisdom to apply the Scriptures. The Holy Spirit will never contradict the Scriptures; He will give you the wisdom to apply His Word.

Paul did preach the gospel to Asia after a few years, when the time was right (see Acts 19:10). Paul also ended up preaching to the whole world – even the world he probably didn't know existed! How? Through his epistles, which were all written chronologically after Acts 16:6-7! What if Paul went to preach in Asia and prematurely died before writing those epistles that are in our New Testament?

The life of Paul communicates to us that although we absolutely need to know the Word of God, we must also know the Spirit of God and learn to be led by Him. The Holy Spirit can lead you in some "out of the box" ways, but it will be for the purpose of maximizing your destiny!

THE JUDGMENT SEAT

It is sobering to think that "We must all appear before the judgment seat of Christ, so that each one may receive what is due for what he has done in the body, whether good or evil" (2 Corinthians 5:10).

When you stand before Jesus, you will be rewarded for the good you've done and subtracted rewards for the bad you've done. But what is considered a "good work"? A good work has to do with the right motives because, apart from love, we gain nothing (1 Corinthians 13:3). Yet additionally, a "good work" has to do with doing what God has ordained us to walk in – our God-given destiny.

> For we are his workmanship, created in Christ Jesus for *good works*, which God prepared beforehand, that we should walk in them.
>
> —Ephesians 2:10

We will not just be rewarded for how love-driven we were, but for how faithful and obedient we were to our God-given destiny. Good motives alone aren't enough. Being a hard worker is not enough; we need to be smart workers who do what the Master says. When you are a smart worker, you will get the most done for our Master. A hard worker who isn't necessarily smart will exert all his energies trying to cut wood with a dull axe. A smart worker will sharpen the axe and get a whole lot more done without the unnecessary striving (see Ecclesiastes 10:10).

Let's be smart workers who walk in what God has prepared for us, not in a bunch of other things that will only burn us out.

BECOME PROPHETIC

You may be saying, "I don't want disorder in my life. I really do want to be a prophetic person and live a Spirit-led life, but where do I start?" It's actually not as hard as you may think.

According to God's Word, you have the ability to hear from God on a regular basis. To say otherwise is either saying Jesus is a liar or you're not saved, because Jesus said, "My sheep hear my voice" (John 10:27). The question is not whether you are able to hear from God but rather, are you taking full advantage of your God-given ability to be led by His voice?

How do we do that?

Let me share with you two simple keys that will jump start you into becoming a prophetic person who clearly and continually hears from God. I'm convinced that a Spirit-led life starts with these two keys. In Matthew 3:16, we see Jesus was filled with the Spirit. In Matthew 4:1, we see that Jesus was led by the Holy Spirit. But I believe that it is in Matthew 3:17 (which bridges Matthew 3:16 and Matthew 4:1) where we find those two vital keys that enable us to go from being just a Spirit-*filled* person (who experienced the infilling of the Holy Spirit) to a Spirit-*led* person (who continually experiences the leading of the Holy Spirit). We learn how to go from being just a person of Pentecost to a person of the prophetic, who knows the voice of God. Both keys are hidden in this verse:

> And behold, a voice from heaven said, "This is my beloved Son, with whom I am well pleased."
>
> —Matthew 3:17

1. Understand You Are a Beloved Child

The first key is to understand that you are a "beloved" child of God. You might wonder, "What does that have to do with me growing as a prophetic person?" Everything.

Do you believe that God loves you enough to speak to you about the details of your life? As a young Christian, that was a pill too big for me to swallow. I didn't understand how the God of the universe could be so in love with me that not only would He save me but also speak to me all the time. Yet, that was my very problem. Our unbelief is the only thing that limits what God wants to do and is willing to do in our lives. It was the unbelief in Nazareth that put a cap on what Jesus could do there (see Mark 6:6).

God is the kind of Father who is actively involved in the lives of His children. Jesus understood that His Father was always willing to show Him what to do. So as He would pray, He would see what His Father wanted Him to do and He did what He saw. Jesus said:

> Truly, truly, I say to you, the Son can do nothing of his own accord, but only what he sees the Father doing. For whatever the Father does, that the Son does likewise.
>
> —John 5:19

Figuratively speaking, Jesus knew that His loving Father was e-mailing Him all the time, so He would constantly check His inbox. Does that describe your walk with God? It can.

2. Understand You Are Pleasing to the Lord

The second key is to understand that you are well pleasing to the Lord. Now you might be thinking, "That is a good key for my self-esteem, but what does it have to do with being led by the Holy Spirit?" Again, everything.

Just like Jesus heard that the Father was well pleased with Him, we need to hear that same truth. It *is* truth. I'm not saying that God has cheered over every decision you've made. We've all made stupid mistakes. Yet, God continually takes pleasure in you. Not everything we've done has been pleasing to Him, but *who we are* is pleasing to Him.

> Having predestinated us unto the adoption of children by Jesus Christ to himself, according to the good plea-sure of his will.
>
> —Ephesians 1:5 KJV

The prodigal son's father was not pleased with all the decisions his foolish son made, but he forever delighted in his boy. This is important because condemnation and shame serve as potent ear-wax that prevents you from receiving the prophetic direction of the Lord.

After a miserable failure is when we need to hear from God the most, so that our lives won't dive into deeper disorder. That is why Satan will fire accusations, telling you that you are unworthy to hear from God anymore (see Revelation 12:10). Satan will try to persuade you that you have no right to pray anymore. Satan will try to convince you to stay out of the presence of God, which is where the voice of God is found. Satan will try to get you to be so self-conscious in shame that you are no longer conscious of the presence and voice of God.

The prophetic works by faith (see Romans 12:6). We must have faith that we are Jesus' sheep who hear our Shepherd's voice. We must have faith that God loves us and delights in us. We must have faith that God desires to speak to us about the details of our lives. We must have faith that when we ask God for wisdom, He will grant wisdom to us.

THE WILDERNESS IS NOT THAT BAD

Jesus firmly believed that He was the beloved and well pleasing Son of God, and that took Him from being just a Spirit-filled Person to a Spirit-led Person. But do you remember where the Holy Spirit first led Him? It wasn't Hawaii or the Bahamas.

> And Jesus, full of the Holy Spirit, returned from the Jordan and was *led by the Spirit in the wilderness for forty days, being tempted by the devil.* And he ate nothing during those days. And when they were ended, he was hungry.
>
> —Luke 4:1-2

Out of all the places that the Holy Spirit could have led Jesus, He led Him to the wilderness to be hammered by temptation; all of this without burgers, pizza, steaks, sweets, coffee, and smoothies.

Are you willing to allow your steps to be ordered of the Lord? If you are, I promise that you will be led to some uncomfortable places. You might be doing things that are seemingly unrelated to your passion and calling (Jesus wasn't called to be isolated in the wilderness). You might be led into spiritual warfare. You might be led to a situation that your body is not happy with. You will face challenges.

However, in the wilderness, Jesus beat up the devil and then returned in the power of the Holy Spirit. And just as Jesus had enough grace to come out on the other side of the wilderness with success and power – you will, too.

Wherever you are in step with the Spirit of grace (Hebrews 10:29), you will have more than enough grace to be super-victorious in all your endeavors! It will be like taking a test with the answers right in front of you. Every fight that God leads you into is a fixed fight. He's already determined that you will come out the winner as long as you cooperate with Him and don't quit! It's the fights that we enter into because of our disobedience that are the real scary ones.

Paul outworked all the other apostles. He would've won "Apostle of the Year" every year. He even wrote, "I worked harder than any of them, though it was not I, but the grace of God that is with me" (1 Corinthians 15:10). Do you know why Paul had the enabling grace of God operating in all his endeavors? He was spiritually keen enough to only fight the battles God led him to. The key to a productive life is doing only that for which God gives you the grace. There is grace for what He orders your steps to do.

We all know that Paul's life and ministry faced one challenge after another – one satanic onslaught after another – but as a man in step with God, he had the grace to be more than a conqueror (Romans 8:37)!

How could Joshua defeat mighty Jericho yet lose to scrawny Ai? On the surface, fighting Jericho was exceedingly more "uncomfortable" than Ai. But Joshua's army didn't have the grace to win over

Ai because at that time they were not in step with the Lord as they were when they defeated Jericho.

Don't make your decisions based on apparent comfort levels. Appearances can be deceiving. Dethrone the idol of comfort, because bowing down to apparent comfort can wreck havoc in your life – just like Ai did to the armies of Israel.

When Israel was devoured by puny Ai, Joshua was in disarray. He felt lost. Yet in the face of his failure, he did the right thing and went to the Lord in prayer, where the Lord explained to him why they couldn't win the battle. The Lord graciously explained why they failed, and Joshua did what the Lord instructed him to do, which included judging Achan. As Joshua obeyed the Lord, disorder turned into order. It's so important to hear and obey the voice of God.

But here is something to consider: if Joshua had sought the Lord beforehand, he would have seen God's red light. Yet, Joshua didn't check for God's red light or green light, because defeating Ai seemed like a walk in the park. That ended up being the worst walk in the park ever. That is why we are called to "walk by faith, not by sight" (2 Corinthians 5:7).

HIS GRACE IS HIDDEN IN HIS WILL

If the Holy Spirit leads you to be a missionary to the Middle East, you will find more success and fulfillment there than anywhere else! Why? His grace or empowerment is hidden in His will. Get a hold of His will and His grace will detonate in and through your life.

In 1991, God spoke to Rick Renner to leave his comfortable home and growing ministry in Oklahoma and move his family to the epicenter of communism – the former Soviet Union.

Communism was still in force, Christians were persecuted by the KGB, the economy was in shambles, and everything looked ghetto. Yet, in obedience to God's leading, he took that great step of faith. Anybody who knows of his ministry is amazed at what the grace of God accomplished through that obedient servant. By God's grace, Rick built the first Christian television network that would blanket the vast land of the former Soviet Union with the Word of God. He has led over a million souls to Christ and pioneered a mega-church. He was able to provide spiritual oversight to hundreds of pastors and a whole lot more.[4]

If you are out of God's will, you may be in the plushest place in the world, with a well-paying job, and leading a seemingly comfortable life, but inside and eventually outside, you will experience disorder.

When God led Israel through the wilderness, He led them with a cloud by day and fire by night. The cloud and fire were Old Testament pictures of the Holy Spirit, who is leading New Testament believers today. Something we need to understand about the cloud and the fire is that if the Israelites were out of step with either one, it would really cost them. As these Israelites traveled on the scorching hot sands of the desert, the only thing that would protect them from melting away was that overshadowing cloud. Deserts are schizophrenic – they are extremely hot in the day but really cold at night. What kept the Israelites warm at night was that overshadowing fire. The Israelites needed to keep in step with the Holy Spirit or they would get lost and really uncomfortable. Ironically, the absolute most comfortable place they could be was in the will of God. It's the same with us.

---

[4] Rick Renner, *If You Were God, Would You Choose You?* (Teach All Nations, March 2006), p.19-20.

WHAT IF A STORM BREAKS OUT?

Jesus told His disciples their immediate destiny: they were going to cross over to the other side. They were led by God to cross the sea. Yet on the way to their destination, there was a ferocious storm! (You can be in step with God and still face storms.) The disciples thought they were going to die in the storm, but Jesus rebuked them for their unbelief and confidently calmed the storm! Sure enough, they got to the other side.

> On that day, when evening had come, he said to them, "Let us go across to the other side." And leaving the crowd, they took him with them in the boat, just as he was. And other boats were with him. And a great windstorm arose, and the waves were breaking into the boat, so that the boat was already filling. But he was in the stern, asleep on the cushion. And they woke him and said to him, "Teacher, do you not care that we are perishing?" And he awoke and rebuked the wind and said to the sea, "Peace! Be still!" And the wind ceased, and there was a great calm. He said to them, "Why are you so afraid? Have you still no faith?" And they were filled with great fear and said to one another, "Who then is this, that even the wind and the sea obey him?"
>
> —Mark 4:35-41

When God speaks to you about your destiny, and you follow the Holy Spirit into it, you will be met by storms. Satan will try to keep you from getting to your God-promised future. Don't freak out like the disciples! Storms are normal. And when things get rough, don't blame God or accuse Him of not caring about you! Trust that He will get you to where He promised! Meanwhile, learn from the example of Jesus and rebuke the storm. Take authority over the devil and never quit. "Resist the devil and he will flee from you" (James 4:7).

If you are on the right track, headed toward your God-ordained destination, although hell may storm against you, there will be more than enough grace to get you to the other side. Remember, there is always grace to get you to your destiny if you are sailing in the right direction.

Jesus knew that He was in the center of God's perfect will, so He was able to sleep through the storm. This speaks of supernatural peace. When you know that you are exactly where God wants you, although storms may come, you can experience supernatural peace during the storms and even take authority over them!

> **Although hell may storm against you, there will be more than enough grace to get you to the other side.**

Don't Go Where It's Convenient

I remember when I was in college, the Lord nudged me to join a church I had visited once called Blessed International Fellowship. But since I lived far away from that church, and they were having three-to-four hour services, I decided that I would go to a church that was closer to my dormitory so I could have more time to do my homework and date my girlfriend (who is now my wife).

So I attended a nearby church for a few months and, although it was a great church, I intuitively knew something was wrong. I felt lost and unfulfilled, and rightfully so. Then one Sunday morning, while I was on my way to this convenient church, the Lord spoke to me again, more authoritatively, and said, "Don't go where it's convenient, go where I send you; I'm sending you to Blessed!"

After I heard the Lord sternly speak to me, I finally obeyed. Blessed wasn't the most comfortable church for me but peace flooded my spirit and, when I was planted there, everything in my life started to fall into place.

> Those that be planted in the house of the LORD shall flourish in the courts of our God.
>
> —Psalm 92:13 KJV

You see, at that stage of my life I had quit pastoral ministry because of discouragement. However, my new pastor, Ryan Lee, kept encouraging me to get back into pastoral ministry and to pursue it full-time. The Lord confirmed Pastor Ryan's advice through profound and powerful Holy Spirit encounters. It was through Blessed that I got back into pastoral ministry and even received the privilege to serve in a full-time capacity, which was my destiny.

Don't get me wrong, there have been challenges, or storms, over the last seven years at Blessed International Fellowship, but I've had overwhelming grace to succeed in this place! I've been able to further develop my gifts, I received promotion after promotion, found many amazing connections, traveled to the nations to preach the gospel, and was ordained as a minister, which were all important components of my divine destiny. I wouldn't have gotten all this at the convenient church.

Have you been filled with the Spirit yet? If so, it's equally important to become a prophetic person. It's understanding that you are the beloved and pleasing child of God that will unlock the prophetic in your life. As a Spirit-filled and Spirit-led person, your life will come into order – and it will be good – real good.

Now that you've been given keys to being led by the Spirit and assured that wherever God leads you, His grace will be there to empower you, let's learn how to thrive in the wilderness, or training camp, in which you are led.

DESTINY QUESTIONS

1. Is there anything you are passionately doing for God, which may not actually be what He has asked you to do?

2. Like Paul, is there anything that the Holy Spirit has specifically forbidden you to do?

3. Do you believe that God loves you and delights in you enough to speak to you about the details of your life?

4. Is there anything God is leading you to do right now that seems uncomfortable? Why should you step out and do it anyway?

CHAPTER FOUR

Thrive In Your Training Camp

G od has a destiny-bridge for you. For Jesus, His time in the wilderness was the necessary bridge to His destiny. God has a wilderness for you. Your wilderness is the training camp that God assigned to you for the purpose of preparing you for your destiny. Where is the training camp that God has assigned you? In His infinite wisdom, He knows which camp would be the absolute best for you. After Jesus came out of the wilderness the Bible tells us:

> And Jesus returned in the *power* of the Spirit to Galilee, and a report about him went out through all the surrounding country.
>
> —Luke 4:14

It's in the wilderness that you are *empowered* to do what you are called to do. It's true that God wants reports about you to spread for His glory, but have you followed Him into the wilderness? Have you cooperated with Him in the wilderness?

Let's talk about your wilderness or training camp.

Not Your Ultimate Calling

Jesus' ultimate calling was not to be isolated in a wilderness. Yet, it was in the wilderness that Jesus was further prepared for His destiny. There will be seasons in your life when the Holy Spirit will lead you to do something that is seemingly not connected to your ultimate calling. However, it will indirectly prepare you for your destiny.

While Moses shepherded sheep for forty years in the wilderness, little did he know that God was preparing him to shepherd three million Israelites. Leading sheep was not the crux of his call, but it was absolutely related to his ultimate destiny.

My first leadership responsibility at Blessed International Fellowship was the Welcoming Ministry. I wondered why my pastor gave me that position since it wasn't my passion, and I wasn't even good at it. This was not my ultimate calling from God, but it did help equip me for what God had prepared for me.

My pastor used to volunteer as the bus driver for his church when he was a college student. Transporting church members in a bus was not his ultimate call, but it equipped him for what God had ultimately prepared for him.

What God has you doing right now in training camp might not be the crux of your calling, but it is actually preparing you for your destiny.

THE PLACE TO SERVE

I've met people who refuse to do anything not directly related to their "calling." I once asked a church member to help us with a particular ministry. She did it grudgingly and told people behind my back that this ministry was not her vision, but Pastor Daniel's. (The truth was that I was just trying to serve the vision of our senior pastors.) That kind of selfish attitude will never set you up for promotion, and destiny is the sum of promotions. If you can't serve another person's vision, you are not ready for your own. As you sow into another's vision with a servant's heart, you are setting yourself up for a harvest with your own vision.

As the Body of Christ, we should all be helping each other fulfill our God-given dreams. The place to start is not to look for people to serve you, but to look for people whom you can serve. Jesus came not to be served, but to serve (see Mark 10:45). He first sowed the seed of selfless serving and today multitudes are serving His vision!

Maybe you don't quite know what you are called to do yet. But if you would just serve someone who does know what they are called to do, and help their vision come to pass, get ready; God will not only give you a vision, but will provide the means to bring your vision to pass.

Never forget that God is moved by and toward someone with a servant's heart.

I remember hearing a powerful testimony from an associate pastor of a church where I once served. He came from a broken home and had major issues with drugs and depression. He got saved and began to serve in his local church. He didn't know what God had called him to do and he lacked confidence. However, he knew that God had called his pastor, and his pastor had a clear vision from

God – so he served his pastor. His servant's heart quickly got him promoted to associate pastor. Finally, he started to see what God had put him on this earth to do. God began to speak to him and his wife about starting a church in San Diego. After many years of being a faithful associate pastor, God opened the door for him, and he is fulfilling God's destiny for his life.

THE PLACE TO BECOME PREGNANT WITH VISION

When Moses was in the wilderness, he was taking care of his father-in-law's sheep. He didn't even have his own business. He was just serving under authority, supporting Jethro's vision. (Jethro was not just Moses' father-in-law; he was also a priest (Jethro is a picture of your spiritual father or mother). Yet it was during Moses' wilderness years that God encountered him powerfully at the burning bush and gave him a vision for his life that would forever change the course of history! So when Moses was commissioned out of the wilderness and sent to Egypt, he wasn't a lost boy but a powerful leader who knew his God and his destiny! Therefore, this man – who was no stranger to shame and failure – was supernaturally empowered to lead an entire nation out of the bondage of slavery!

The wilderness is your time to encounter God like never before and receive clear blueprints for your life!

This is why it's stupid to skip or prematurely ditch the wilderness; God desires to encounter you in the wilderness and impregnate you with His vision so you can be the world-class leader He's called you to be. Don't ever get weary in the wilderness just because you aren't doing what you are ultimately most passionate about. It's your time to serve your Jethro's vision, to encounter God like never before, and receive clear blueprints for your life from God Himself!

THE PLACE TO WIN SECRET BATTLES

The greatest blessings I received during my years at Blessed International Fellowship were not just the public victories, but also the private victories. The wilderness is a place where you win secret battles! It's the place where you come face-to-face with your devils (the ones that you had been living with for years) and triumph over them! In the pattern of Jesus, it's only after we have beat up the devil in private that we are ready to beat him up in public.

I had a number of issues when I came to Blessed. Two of the biggest issues were a spirit of fear and a spirit of rebellion. I was such a timid person in social interactions that I was socially awkward. I picked up a spirit of rebellion through deep disappointments in my previous pastors. When someone in authority asked me to do something, the rebel in me would arise, and I no longer wanted to do it. That was a satanic, rebellious spirit at work. The way we treat our pastors reflects our heart toward God. Let me explain: a basketball coach appoints the starting point guard to be the team captain. The other players are to follow his lead. If the other four players on the court decide they will play however they want, they are not just dishonoring the point guard, but the coach. God has appointed your pastor. Get the point?

As I started serving at Blessed, I found myself prone to distrust pastors. One day while I was at a Christian bookstore, I saw a book titled *Honor's Reward* by John Bevere. For the first time in my life, I heard the Holy Spirit tell me to buy and read a Christian book. As I read that book, I felt like surgery was taking place in my heart. It led me to deep repentance and awesome deliverance. I realized how my past hurts had paralyzed me from honoring others as I should have. I was so convicted that I started phoning people and meeting up with others just to repent for my lack of honor. I even had this awkward talk with my dad and repented for my lack of honor. Then I went to my pastor and repented for not honoring him as I should, and something broke off of me! Again, I wouldn't have gotten this at the convenient church.

Recently, I preached this message, "Thrive in Your Training Camp," at our church. Afterward, my pastor shared with the congregation that when I repented for the spirit of rebellion and expressed my desire to honor him, his heart melted and something shifted in our entire church. Our personal victories have a real ripple effect.

Many future world-changers come to their assigned wilderness with their unresolved father issues, rejection issues, and the list goes on. Their wilderness is the very time and place to get free!

Maybe when you joined the church that God sent you to, you suddenly began to wrestle with all these strange feelings and thoughts. It's because it's the time and place for them to be uprooted!

In the wilderness, God is not wasting your time; He's preparing you for your destiny. How well you do with your private battles will determine how well you do with your public battles. Jesus said, "One who is faithful in a very little is also faithful in much, and one who is dishonest in a very little is also dishonest in much" (Luke 16:10).

Remember, David killed the lions and bears in the wilderness before taking down Goliath and before he walked into his kingly destiny. Many of God's people don't want to kill their lions and bears in the wilderness, yet they want to face Goliath and be king overnight. Prematurely ditching your wilderness will leave you lost.

Now think about this: if you absolutely stink in your wilderness, why do you think you are ready to thrive in your Promised Land? That's ridiculous. I told one zealous young man, "If you can't rise to be an honorable leader here in our church, how can you be the world-class leader God has destined you to be?" Jesus told the disciples that they would take Jerusalem and Judea first before tackling the ends of the earth (Acts 1:8-9). If you can't be promoted in your wilderness, forget the Promised Land!

THE PLACE TO BREAK FAMILY CURSES

Satan had a sneaking suspicion that Jesus was the last Adam, who had come to bring restoration of the mess that the first Adam had gotten humanity into. Therefore, Satan tried to gun Jesus down with the same kind of temptations that He fired at Adam and Eve. So in the wilderness, Jesus had to undo the mess of the previous generations. He was known as the "Son of David"—David was a man who crumbled before temptation—Jesus had to break off the long-existing pattern of failure so He could start a new order.

Maybe you come from a long line of alcoholics – it's time for you to break free and start a new order! Perhaps you come from a long line of infidelity – it's time for you to break free and start a new order! If you come from a long line of poverty, it's time for you to break free and start a new world order!

In your wilderness, which is the place you are sent by the Holy Spirit, you get to break generational curses and cast out family devils that are aiming to shoot you down. Don't get scared of the flying bullets; remember that if God led you to it, He will lead you through it! His grace is there. His grace is more than enough.

THE PLACE TO LEARN SKILL IN THE WORD

Many would rather skip the wilderness and just step into their destiny, yet it's the wilderness that equips you for your destiny! Those who aren't led by the Spirit will jump the gun and ditch their wilderness, only to find their lives in disorder.

The apostle Paul spent years in the wilderness, throwing off old mindsets and smashing devils under his feet until he was ready for his destiny (see Galatians 1:17)!

It was in the wilderness where Jesus learned to skillfully use the sword of the Word of God against the devil. After Jesus pounded on the devil with the Word of God, the enemy left with his tail between his legs. The devil left and angels came. Sounds like a good transaction to me. If you are in the wilderness, get ready for that very transaction!

The wilderness is a time to equip yourself with the Word of God. The investment of time in God's Word enables us to "be complete, equipped for every good work" (2 Timothy 3:17). Right now might be the opportune time for you to spend hours a day in the Scriptures, because the time will come when you won't have that same luxury. I'm not saying we ever outgrow the need to spend time in the Word, but I hope you get my point.

You can earn five doctorates in counseling, but nothing will equip you to change the world like spending time in the Word of God! It is the sword of the Spirit (see Ephesians 6:17)!

It's in the wilderness that you become skilled with the sword of God's Word. It's in the wilderness you learn to cast out devils as you fight spiritual warfare. It's in the wilderness you grow sensitive to the supernatural world. It's in the wilderness you learn to preach yourself out of discouragement and into the anointing! It's in the wilderness you learn to teach yourself out of confusion into clarity!

It's in the wilderness you go from faith to faith, revelation to revelation, and become equipped for your destiny!

COOPERATE IN THE WILDERNESS OR DIE THERE

Jesus was only in the wilderness for forty days, and He came out with power and favor to live out His destiny. The Israelites were in the wilderness for forty years, and most of them died there. How long do you want to be in your training camp? Do you want to ultimately be released into your destiny or do you want to die in your training camp?

> In the wilderness, you can either have your heart further melted by God, or hardened by rebellion and pride.

It's not enough to be led by the Spirit into the wilderness of God's choice; you must be willing to ebb and flow with Him in the wilderness if you want to get through it. There is more than enough grace for you to conquer the oppositions of the enemy in the wilderness, but if you choose to disconnect and disagree with the Holy Spirit while you are there, you will die in the wilderness or the wilderness will kill you.

Out of the millions of Israelites who were obedient enough to get into the training camp, only Joshua and Caleb got to walk into their destiny, which was the Promised Land. The rest died in the wilderness because of their refusal to cooperate with God. In the wilderness, you can either have your heart further melted by God or further hardened by rebellion and pride.

Where is your wilderness? Where is the place God has sent you to be trained for your future? Have you refused to deal with your issues and break free from them? Are you foolishly demoting yourself and refusing to grow up? Do you constantly point the finger of accusations upon others while failing to see that you are the one who really needs to change?

Always accusing others is not evidence of how prophetic you are; quite the opposite is true. It only exposes how blind you are to your own issues (see Matthew 7:3). The wilderness is the place to overcome our own issues, not call out everyone else's.

The wilderness is a place of pruning, and if you are cooperating with the Holy Spirit, that's exactly what will happen! When I first was given a little bit of responsibility at Blessed, I was quite flaky or unreliable. I didn't know how to show up to meetings on time, I wouldn't meet deadlines, and I'd say one thing but do something else. I knew God was determined to burn the flakiness out of me, and I cooperated. I went from being an unreliable person to a dependable pastor. If I stayed flaky in my wilderness, I would have died a flake! Flakiness would have assassinated my destiny. What does God want to burn out of you? Are you cooperating? Too much is at stake.

Learn from history: if you rebel in the wilderness, you will die there! Remember, you have all the grace you need to succeed in the wilderness or your training camp, so don't waste that grace – use it.

DESTINY ON A SILVER PLATTER?

No one in his right mind will give a shotgun to a two-year-old. Paul warned Timothy to not give big responsibilities to new believers because "he may become puffed up with conceit and fall into the condemnation of the devil" (1 Timothy 3:6). Paul additionally warns Timothy not to appoint leaders suddenly (1 Timothy 5:22).

That on-fire, new believer can very well be called and destined to be a great leader with global responsibilities, but Paul made it clear that if he is promoted too quickly, he will fall into the condemnation of the devil. That's serious. Destiny is not handed on a silver platter right away, no more than a pistol is given to a preschooler.

What is the condemnation of the devil? When God promoted Lucifer and gave him increased influence, Lucifer turned proud and began to despise the very One who raised him up. When Satan possessed Judas, he made Judas turn his back on the very One who chose him, taught him, fed him, trained him, and discipled him.

I've seen anointed new believers promoted too quickly, only to see their nasty egos inflate so big that they are no longer teachable. Deceived, they think they are more spiritual than their pastor who poured into them, laid down their lives for them, and foolishly raised them up too soon!

Whenever you see people despise the very leader who increased their influence, that is the definition of satanic! That is why destiny cannot come to you on a silver platter. God wants to burn away any kind of resemblance to Satan in us so that when we receive promotion, we manifest the Lamb of God, not Lucifer. According to Paul, it takes time for God to burn away that satanic pride. That is why it takes time to possess your Promised Land. That is why we need training camp.

The reason God didn't allow the Israelites to walk straight into their Promised Land – or destiny – was that they wouldn't be strong enough to sustain it if it was given to them on a silver platter!

> I will not drive them out from before you in one year, lest the land become desolate and the wild beasts multiply against you. Little by little I will drive them out from before you, until you have increased and possess the land.
>
> —Exodus 23:29-30

This is why God will assign you to your training ground where you will have the opportunity to win the little victories. That's how you will increase in faith, character, patience, wisdom, and love enough to not just possess but to sustain your destiny.

Unlike Moses, David, Paul, or Jesus, King Saul never had a training camp. He never ate humble pie in the wilderness. He was crowned as king overnight. This wasn't God's perfect will, but the product of human foolishness (see 1 Samuel 8:7). So Saul came into office with all his junk. His pride only grew like weeds while he was on the throne. While he enjoyed doing religious activities, Saul's pride choked out his heart for God. His pride conceived many children: bitterness, rebellion toward authority, disobedience, self-righteousness, and more. When a person is promoted too soon, like Saul, he or she can care more about their reputation before men than their relationship with God.

Since Saul didn't learn the art of repentance in training camp, he only hardened his heart. Since he didn't learn how to overcome sin, he only got deeper into it. Therefore, Samuel told him:

> You have done foolishly. You have not kept the command of the LORD your God, with which he commanded you. For then the LORD *would have* established your kingdom over Israel forever.
>
> —1 Samuel 13:13

Samuel tells Saul of what *would have* been. There are many "would have, could have, and should have beens." They fell short of their potential and squandered their destiny.

In training camp, we develop a heart for the Lord, not just for success. We become purified before promotion, so we won't be another "would have been."

Now in a great house there are not only vessels of gold and silver but also of wood and clay, some for honorable use, some for dishonorable. Therefore, if anyone cleanses himself from what is dishonorable, he will be a vessel for honorable use, set apart as holy, useful to the master of the house, ready for every good work.

—2 Timothy 2:20-21

This passage does not prove that some Christians are destined for greatness while others aren't. It teaches that if we want to reach our great destiny, we need to cleanse ourselves from the sin and weight that desires to entangle us. The Scriptures say, "Let us lay aside every weight, and the sin which doth so easily beset us, and let us run with patience the race that is set before us" (Hebrews 12:1 KJV). Training camp is prime time for this.

DON'T GET BITTER

The wilderness is not the place to get bitter. If you ever get bitter, your God-ordained training camp will become your torturous concentration camp! Don't let that happen to you. Don't die in the wilderness.

If there is anyone in the Bible who knew the temptation to get bitter, it was Joseph. He was betrayed by his brothers and sold into slavery by his own flesh and blood. Potipher's wife falsely accused him of trying to rape her when she was the seductress. He was fired and sent to prison because he did the right thing to not sin against Potipher and God. Joseph could've been one angry prisoner, but he chose not to get bitter in prison.

The prison was not Joseph's destiny – it was a destiny bridge; it was his training camp, or his wilderness. The bridges to your destiny may not always glitter, but they will surely connect you if you stay on the course.

One day Joseph met Pharaoh's ex-baker and ex-butler who had both been fired and thrown into prison. With a servant's heart, Joseph reached out to them and discovered that they both had disturbing dreams, which Joseph interpreted. Joseph didn't have to extend himself, yet he was willing. Joseph could have been bitter at God and said, "I'm not going to use the gifts You've given me anymore! I'm mad at You! To hell with all the people!" If Joseph had responded that way, he would have died in prison!

SERVE UNDER SUPERVISION

Joseph served under the warden. Whom has God called you to serve under? If God has connected you to a particular church to be trained, with a servant's heart use your God-given gifts under the supervision of your pastors/leaders. That's important.

> Obey your leaders and submit to them, for they are keeping watch over your souls, as those who will have to give an account. Let them do this with joy and not with groaning, for that would be of no advantage to you.
>
> —Hebrews 13:17

Joseph served so well that the warden promoted him to become the CEO of operations (see Genesis 39:22), which was perfect training for the young man who would serve as the CEO of the largest "Feed the World" enterprise the world had ever seen.

If you don't like serving under supervision, you are proud and arrogant, and God opposes the proud (see James 4:6, 1 Peter 5:5). If you don't like serving under authority, you might have a call to be a prophet to the world, but your sphere of influence will not extend past the church parking lot. Nobody (including God) will trust you with a church pulpit. Although you have gifts and callings, you will lack character and credibility. And what good is your potential if you don't even have a platform?

- Joshua's character and credibility came from serving under Moses, a credible leader.

- Samuel's character and credibility came from serving under Eli, the anointed priest.

- David's character and credibility came from serving under Saul, the appointed king.

- Elisha's character and credibility came from serving under Elijah, the prophet of God.

- Timothy's character and credibility came from serving under Paul, the apostle.

Have you ever served under a God-ordained minister or ministry? If not, no wonder your character is lacking and your credibility is uncertain. The wilderness is the breeding ground for your character and credibility; they will both converge to create a good name and favor. "A good name is to be chosen rather than great riches, and favor is better than silver or gold" (Proverbs 22:1).

Just as Joseph made the warden's job easier, use your gifts and make the pastor's job easier. You aren't just helping the church; you are developing your own potential, credibility, and platform.

If God has led you to work somewhere with a servant's heart and your God-given gifts, make your boss's job easier. You aren't just helping the business; you're helping yourself! You are being prepared for your destiny as a CEO of your own business. Before you know it, promotion after promotion will come your way! *Destiny is the sum of promotions.*

PERFECT YOUR GIFTS

Just because you aren't in the center of your destiny doesn't mean you shouldn't use your gifts. No! Rather, perfect your gifts! If you get discouraged and bitter in your training camp and stop using the natural and spiritual gifts God has given you, Satan has you where he wants you.

When Joseph used his natural gifts, he became very successful in the prison. And as Joseph used his spiritual gift (of dream interpretation), he got out of prison and into his destiny. How well you develop your gifts while in training camp will determine how much influence you will ultimately create for yourself!

A man's gift makes room for him and brings him before the great.

—Proverbs 18:16

A dull axe head will not be as efficient as a sharp one (see Ecclesiastes 10:10). Your time in training camp is your time to sharpen your axe (your gifts). Even when no one invited me to preach, I would spend countless hours sharpening my axe! Every time I work on a new book, I'm sharpening my axe! What are you doing to sharpen your gifts?

Joseph used his gifts as a volunteer! When you are only willing to use your gifts if you are paid for your services, you aren't getting the most out of your training ground. If the church insists on paying you, that's one thing; but if you are demanding payment for your services, that's another thing. That is not a servant's heart, which is imperative to promotion. Freely sow your gift and reap your destiny.

While young David was in the wilderness, he perfected his gift of playing the harp. So when King Saul sought someone to play music that would hush the evil spirits that tormented him, he was introduced to David (see 1 Samuel 16:15-18). David then became the king's armor bearer, which was another stepping stone toward his destiny. Serving as Saul's armor bearer gave him the opportunity to defeat Goliath, which was the next stepping stone toward his destiny. Killing Goliath gave David the opportunity to be one of the generals in the army; one more stepping stone toward his destiny. Finally, David became king, but his initial entrance into the palace all started with his developed gift.

Meet Your Divine Connections

If you don't get bitter, God's grace will be there to make you highly successful in your training camp; the camp will get the most out of you and you out of it. But if you do get bitter, that grace (or divine enablement to succeed) that is available for you will vaporize.

> See to it that no one fails to obtain the grace of God; that no "root of bitterness" springs up and causes trouble, and by it many become defiled.
>
> —Hebrews 12:15

Bitterness will suck out your joy, which is your divine strength (see Nehemiah 8:10). But as you maintain a sweet spirit, the grace of God will enable you to thrive and you will be divinely connected to your destiny. Joseph couldn't have reached his destiny if it wasn't for his prison time, because it was in prison where Joseph ministered to Pharaoh's ex-butler. And it was that ex-butler who eventually ended up connecting Joseph to his destiny.

Joseph was keen enough to see that this ex-butler would play an important role in his destiny. Therefore, after interpreting his dream, Joseph told him, "Only remember me, when it is well with you, and please do me the kindness to mention me to Pharaoh, and so get me out of this house" (Genesis 40:14).

Joseph's interpretations proved to be spot on. Just as he had prophesied, the ex-butler got restored to office! And sure enough, after a few years, Pharaoh had a distressing dream. That's when his butler introduced him to Joseph! See that chain of events? This is how destiny happens.

> Until the time came to fulfill his dreams, the Lord tested Joseph's character.
>
> —Psalm 105:19 NLT

When you are in the right training camp, serving under supervision, developing and sowing your gifts, you will meet the right people – your divine connections – and your divine connections will connect you to your destiny.

Like Joseph, you can even have the spiritual perception to recognize your divine connections as long as you don't get bitter.

Now let's take a closer look at what divine connections are and how we are to relate to them.

DESTINY QUESTIONS

1. Where has God stationed you to be trained?

2. What does God desire to burn out of you? Are there sins or weights in your life that you need to shake off? What are they?

3. What are the natural and spiritual gifts that God has given to you? Are you using them with a servant's heart and developing your gifts under supervised authority?

CHAPTER FIVE

Honor Divine Connections

We will meet thousands of people throughout our lifetime. Some of those people have been sent by the devil to ruin your life and destiny, while others have been appointed by God to bless your life and connect you to your destiny. Are you rightfully discerning who is who?

King Saul did not honor his divine connection – his armor-bearer, David. David was Saul's greatest asset. He was everything Saul wasn't. David had the utmost love and respect for Saul and more importantly, David had the anointing to set Saul free from his tormenting evil spirits. Yet, because of Saul's insecurities, he turned on David and tried to kill him.

I've seen God connect broken Sauls with godly Davids (an anointed church, a loving pastor, a Spirit-filled ministry, a good friend), but because their insecurities blind them from recognizing their divine connection, they kill that connection. Satan will try to make you suspicious of your Davids.

Satan tried using my past hurts to cause me to distrust the Davids God brought into my life. Then Holy Spirit rebuked me and helped me discern my Davids, the ones He had brought into my life to support me and set me free. Allow the Holy Spirit to help you see through the cloud of your insecurity and past hurts so you can honor your divine connections.

I've watched people marry their diabolical connections and "kill" their divine connections. They get intimate with their Delilahs but reject their Davids. As a result, their destinies went down the toilet.

I can think of a man who was doing excellent in the ministry as an associate pastor. In our conversations together, he clearly articulated when, where, and how God called him to be a pastor! Yet, he entered into a relationship with a girl who thought he shouldn't pursue ministry. She turned his heart against his pastor, who was his divine connection. Eventually, he married this girl, and he is out of the ministry today.

While we are called to love everyone, we aren't to connect with everyone. You need to join with whom God has divinely connected you.

Who Is Your Eli?

Everyone wants to be a hero. Do you know that God wants you to be a hero, too? He desires His people to be the head and not the tail; at the top and never at the bottom (see Deuteronomy

28:13). He desires that we shine as stars and bring glory to our Father through our lives (see Matthew 5:16).

Prophet Samuel was a true hero, a shining star. Samuel was used by God to bring revival to his nation. He preached one sermon and the nation repented (see 1 Samuel 7:3-4). God so honored Samuel that God didn't let any of his words go unfulfilled (see 1 Samuel 3:19). For thousands of years, people have gleaned from the wisdom and life of Samuel. Yet, I'm thankful that the Scriptures take us through the "making of the prophet," not just his glamour shots.

Samuel spent years assisting Eli, the High Priest. Eli was Samuel's divine connection – the bridge to his destiny. Although Eli was a legitimate servant of God, he was far from perfect. He failed to discipline his sons and they were thorns to Eli's reputation. He also failed to discipline himself, and he was obese. Yet the call and anointing of God rested upon Eli.

Samuel wasn't wasting his time as he assisted the High Priest. The Bible tells us that he was actually serving the Lord while assisting Eli (see 1 Samuel 3:1 NLT). I've assisted my church and pastor for about seven years, but I know Whom I was *really* serving all along! Therefore, my reward ultimately comes from Him. When we understand this reality, it will change our attitude. Paul wrote to those who were working and serving under authority to "Serve wholeheartedly, as if you were serving the Lord, not men" (Ephesians 6:7 NIV).

Who is your Eli? Your Eli is who, where, and how God has called you to serve Him right now.

It was under Eli that Samuel was trained for his destiny. Samuel was destined to be a prophet and it was while he served Eli that he learned to hear the voice of God. Eli helped Samuel to hear the voice of God, which was directly related to developing Samuel's gift of prophecy and calling as a prophet (see 1 Samuel 3:9). While you serve under your appointed Eli, he will help you discover and develop your individual gifts and callings!

Now, do you really think that Samuel and Eli always got along? Don't you imagine that Samuel had his share of disagreements with Eli? Maybe Samuel thought Eli was too old-school, too undisciplined, etc. Perhaps Eli thought Samuel was just a kid and didn't give him the respect that Samuel desired. Yet, not once do we see Samuel dishonor his pastor! Disagreements are not dangerous (since they can refine our beliefs), but to dishonor your divine connection is lethal to your destiny!

Your Eli may be your current pastor, boss, or ministry in which God has divinely connected you. Your Eli will not always be perfect toward you. Be warned: you will be able to find flaws with your divine connection. Will you continue to serve with honor like Samuel, or will you jump ship over petty offenses. Beware! That other ship you foolishly jump into might not be sailing to your destiny.

Maybe God has revealed that you will have your own business, church, ministry, organization, television show, etc., but remember that Jesus said, "And if you have not been faithful in that which is another's, who will give you that which is your own?" (Luke 16:12).

Disagreements are not dangerous, but to dishonor your divine connection is lethal to your destiny!

If you cannot be diligent serving another person's business or ministry, what makes you think you will be diligent when you run your own? According to Jesus, you're crazy if you think so.

LEARN OR REPEAT

If Samuel made one mistake in his life, it was that he failed to learn from Eli's mistakes. It turned out that Samuel also failed to discipline his sons (see 1 Samuel 8:1-3). God connected you to your Eli so you would learn from his or her mistakes, not repeat them!

I know of a famous minister who, as a young man, was divinely connected to a woman with a powerful healing ministry. It's truly apparent that he received an impartation from sitting under her ministry. This woman minister did not have the best people skills; she would snap at people and yell at those who served under her ministry. This young man was startled when he saw her act that way! But after years of sitting under that behavior, he got used to it and picked it up himself.

When someone you respect has flaws, make sure you don't eat the bones along with the meat. Please digest the meat, but spit out the bones!

The best way to learn is not from your mistakes, but the mistakes of *others*. That is why God will connect you to your Eli – to learn from their mistakes! It's imperative that you learn in an honorable way. If you are quick to expose the nakedness of your spiritual father, your divine connection, you are following in the way of Noah's son, Ham, who exposed his dad's nakedness instead of covering it. Ham's dishonorable attitude brought a curse upon his destiny (see Genesis 9:20-28).

David highly respected his predecessor, King Saul, but after David sinned he made sure that he didn't follow in the unrepentant ways of Saul, and he repented wholeheartedly (see Psalm 51). David witnessed how Saul was demonized through his progression into greater sin, so he did everything he could to avoid Saul's fate.

Thankfully, David was able to learn from the tragedy of Saul losing the anointing, and David was able to protect his destiny.

I'm not saying that we are called to blindly follow and mindlessly agree with everything our pastor, church, or ministry decides. Disagreeing here and there is fine; dishonor isn't. "Honor everyone" (1 Peter 2:17).

If your pastor becomes a cult leader or lives in terrible sin, obviously you need to get out of there! "We must obey God rather than men" (Acts 5:29). But if you disconnect yourself from your divine connection because his personality rubs you the wrong way ... she was seemingly rude to you ... you don't feel treasured by them ... or your pride tells you that you are now more spiritual than they are... you might be detouring your own destiny!

It's not that we depend on people to make destiny happen for us; we know to look to God as our source. But to honor and faithfully serve those with whom God has divinely connected us, is a bridge to destiny.

HONOR – THE KEY TO A PROSPEROUS LIFE

One day the Holy Spirit took me to the following passage and explained it to me:

> "Honor your father and mother" – which is the first commandment with a promise – "that it may go well with you and that you may enjoy long life on the earth."
>
> —Ephesians 6:2-3 NIV

Of course I had read this passage many times, but through this conversation with the Holy Spirit, I received a much deeper understanding and appreciation of its meaning. The Holy Spirit explained how honoring parents leads to a prosperous life. He first explained that children have a malleable heart (see Proverbs 22:6). Therefore, when a young child makes decisions to dishonor his parents, he becomes conditioned to dishonor. So as he grows up and goes to school, he is prone to dishonor his teachers, making him a bad student. When he makes friends, he lacks the basic skill of honoring them, making him a bad friend. When he gets a job, he doesn't know how to truly honor his boss, making him a lousy employee. If he starts a business, his employees will not be happy with him. He can even join a church but will have tendencies to dishonor his pastor, causing his church-life to suffer. When he marries and has children, his family-life will be a struggle since he has only fortified his dishonoring ways.

This is how devastating dishonor can be.

But that is all turned around for a child who has been conditioned to honor. He will grow to do well in school, with friends, at his job, in his business, in his church, and with his family. In other words, he will live a long, happy, prosperous life. This is how important it is to have a heart of honor; it will affect almost every area of our lives. Therefore, honor determines your destiny.

HONOR – THE KEY TO EVER-INCREASING REVIVAL

God's will for His Church is that every generation goes from glory to glory – period. So why does it seem that most revivals usually don't last for even one generation? One of the main reasons is the lack of honor.

When God commanded the Israelites to honor their fathers and mothers, it was to literally keep the land. This is how the Israelites understood this commandment to honor parents: if a son was willing to honor his father and mother enough to take care of them in their old age, they were given their parent's property in exchange.[5] Therefore, for Israel to keep the land of their fathers, the culture of honor was a necessity. As you honored your parents enough to take care of them, the property that they inherited or fought for became your inheritance.

The same is true in the spiritual realm. If we want to inherit the blessing, wisdom, prosperity, and anointing of our spiritual fathers and mothers, we must honor them. We can't keep fighting for land that's already been won. We can't keep reinventing the wheel every generation.

When Elisha asked his spiritual father, Elijah, for the double-portion of his anointing, Elijah said that he had asked for a difficult thing. Not because it's difficult for God to give it; it's difficult for people to receive it.

Elijah told Elisha that if he saw him taken up, the double portion would be his. Afterward, Elijah did everything he could to shake Elisha loose. He purposefully offended him left and right. Yet Elisha passed the test of honor, and when Elijah was caught up, Elisha cried out, "My father! My father!" and tore his clothes in sorrow (see 2 Kings 2:12). Elisha possessed the inheritance of Elijah because he honored and loved Elijah as a father. Elisha didn't

---

[5] "Ancient Near Eastern legal documents make children's right to inherit their parents' property contingent on honoring them by providing and caring for them. Here God applies this condition on a national scale: the right of future generations of Israelites to inherit the land of Israel from their parents is contingent upon honoring them" (Jewish Study Bible, Oxford, p. 150). For this reason, I don't believe you can have twenty spiritual fathers and thirty spiritual mothers. You cannot care for that many people. I personally believe you can have no more than five. You can have many teachers and mentors but not fathers and mothers (see 1 Corinthians 4:15).

have the attitude, "Yes! Elijah's out of the picture, I'm the superstar now!" He didn't see Elijah as a stepping stone or a sugar daddy, but a real father. Double portions belong to good sons.

Jesus confirmed that honor was the key to receiving the inheritance: "The one who receives a prophet because he is a prophet will receive a prophet's reward, and the one who receives a righteous person because he is a righteous person will receive a righteous person's reward" (Matthew 10:41). The prophet and righteous person's reward involves receiving what they carry. I can't reward you with a helicopter because I don't have one. Through honor, we can possess what a man or woman of God possesses.

Jesus is salvation, but how did we access His salvation? By honoring Him as our Savior and Lord. Honor brings access. Jesus' hometown, Nazareth, couldn't access the miracle-working power that was upon Jesus, because they did not honor Him (see Matthew 13:53-58).

When there is dishonor between children and their parents, the Scriptures warn that the land will be struck with a curse (see Malachi 4:6). The land that the previous generation fought for and inherited will be inaccessible to the dishonoring generation. If we want to see an ever-increasing revival, with a heart of honor we must inherit the real estate of wisdom, anointing, faith, glory, etc., of our spiritual mothers and fathers. Only through honor can their ceiling can be our floor.

HONOR – A KEY TO PROMOTION

Promotion comes from God (see Psalm 75:6-7). Destiny is the sum of promotions. It's possible for us to waste our potential and destroy our destinies because God cannot promote us.

When Samuel saw handsome Eliab (David's oldest brother), he was convinced that this man was to be the next king. Yet God rebuked Samuel, saying, "Do not look on his appearance or on the height of his stature, because I have rejected him. For the LORD sees not as man sees: man looks on the outward appearance, but the LORD looks on the heart" (1 Samuel 16:7). Samuel ends up anointing the overlooked David to be king.

Why did God reject Eliab? It was because of pride (see James 4:6).

In the next chapter, we see the manifestation of Eliab's pride. When his youngest brother David was sent by his father to bring bread to his brothers, David began asking the other men what the reward would be for the man who defeats Goliath.

> When Eliab, David's oldest brother, heard him speaking with the men, he burned with anger at him and asked, "Why have you come down here? And with whom did you leave those few sheep in the desert? I know how conceited you are and how wicked your heart is; you came down only to watch the battle."
>
> —1 Samuel 17:28 NIV

This is pride in action. First, Eliab said that David had only a "few sheep in the desert," implying that he was insignificant. Second, Eliab accused David of being proud and evil. Proud people see other people as insignificant in comparison to them. Proud people have critical spirits and angrily accuse other people. God cannot use people like this.

Compare Eliab with David. David submitted to his father, served his brothers, and asked questions. That's the heart of humility.

Humility and honor are inseparable. That's why God promoted David to be king.

Proud people don't submit to their spiritual fathers; they do whatever they feel like doing. Proud people don't serve their brothers; they usually isolate themselves or just use people. Proud people don't ask questions; they just want to preach and teach.

> A man's pride will bring him low, But a humble spirit will obtain honor.
>
> —Proverbs 29:23 NASB

Are You a Kisser or a Cleaver?

Faithfulness is an expression of honor.

Naomi had a loving husband and two sons who had wives. Then tragedy struck Naomi's life, and her beloved husband and her prized sons all passed away suddenly! Naomi was now left with her two daughters-in-law, Orpah and Ruth (see Ruth 1).

Naomi was Orpah and Ruth's divine connection, their spiritual mother. God brought Naomi into their lives to lead them first to God and secondly into their God-given destinies. (Coming to saving faith in God is the starting point for living out our God-given destiny.)

Due to the hardships that bombarded Naomi, she changed her name from Naomi to Mara – Naomi means pleasant, while Mara means bitter.

> She said to them, "Do not call me Naomi; call me Mara, for the Almighty has dealt very bitterly with me."
>
> —Ruth 1:20

Naomi even instructed her daughters-in-law to leave her and go find themselves husbands who would take care of them. This sounded good to Orpah, so she deserted Naomi with a kiss. But Ruth clung to her divine connection!

> And Orpah kissed her mother-in-law, but Ruth clung to her.
>
> —Ruth 1:14

To make a long story short, it was through Naomi that faithful Ruth was able to meet a man named Boaz, a godly millionaire with an awesome personality (not a bad combination, right ladies?). Boaz and Ruth got married, and they lived happily ever after, having kids, grandkids, and great grandkids, which included King David and eventually King Jesus!

I doubt that Boaz ever had to question Ruth's faithfulness since he saw for himself how Ruth dealt with Naomi. Jesus said, "One who is faithful in a very little is also faithful in much, and one who is dishonest in a very little is also dishonest in much" (Luke 16:10).

Boaz was Ruth's destiny! We all would like to marry our Boaz (so to speak); but God asks, "How are you doing with your Naomi? Are you a kisser or a cleaver?"

You will see your divine connection go through pleasant times and also some bitter times; will you kiss your divine connection goodbye, or wisely cleave?

The Scriptures never speak of Orpah again. Kissers never make history, but those who have the character to cleave to their divine connection leave their imprint through time.

When I first joined the staff at Blessed International Fellowship, the ministry was very pleasant. It was growing fast and the presence of God was gloriously thick! Then our church went through a really tough stretch for about three years. During this trying time, many of our staff members kissed the church goodbye because it seemed like the smart thing to do. Some thought that they should just link up with bigger, more promising ministries. But I knew in my spirit that this church was my divine connection, so I cleaved.

After about three years of famine, an amazing shift took place. Seasons changed! People joined the church, miracles started to happen, lives began to change, and finances flowed. I honestly feel bad for all the Orpahs, because if they had only cleaved to their Naomi, they would have met their Boaz.

I'm aware that not everyone's situation is the same. I'm not saying that you must stick with your current church if they teach heresy, or to stay committed to your pastor even when he is having an illicit affair, or to hold onto a ministry that God is clearly calling you to let go of. But you must not cut loose just because the ministry you've been assigned to hits a rough patch.

Don't be an overly sensitive, emotional baby who is easily hurt and breaks fellowship over insignificant things. Please, for your destiny's sake, don't be a coward who runs from inconvenience. For the sake of those people that need you to fulfill destiny, don't be a church-hopper, pastor-swapper, and anointing connoisseur who has something to say about every church and ministry but doesn't know how to faithfully serve in rain or shine!

FAITHFULNESS PAYS BIG

Before God will bless you with your Boaz, He will test you with your Naomi. In high school, I had a good friend who also wanted to be in full-time pastoral ministry. While my God-given dream was primarily preaching and teaching, his God-given dream had to do with worship leading and recording CDs. God had him serving at his father's church, which was very small and seemingly insignificant. Week in and week out, my friend led worship on his guitar for six people – two were the pastors on staff, one was his sister, and the others were just kids with no heart to worship God – yet, he stuck with it! After he was faithful to his Naomi for five years, he met his Boaz!

Out of the blue, a youth pastor invited my friend to join him in planting a church. My friend's father knew that this was God rewarding his son for his faithfulness and so released him to go. It turned out that this church plant became one of the fastest growing churches in California, with a huge vision for their worship ministry. They've recorded many anointed worship CDs, and guess who is the main songwriter and singer for all those tracks? Faithfulness pays big!

Don't Despise Small Beginnings

Faithfulness is the route to fulfilling destiny. Flaky people don't fulfill destiny, they only envy, criticize, or worship those who do.

When I met my wife, I didn't really know what her unique destiny was. She had a heart for God but didn't know what God had specifically called her to do. She wanted to serve God so she volunteered with the toddlers ministry. Due to her servant's heart, she soon became the director. Now, the Toddlers Ministry is not easy at any church, but it was especially challenging at Blessed International Fellowship – services went over three hours, and we had up to eight major conferences every year when services would go from four to six hours every night.

Despite the temptation, my wife chose not to complain. She wasn't getting paid either, nor expecting to get paid in the future; she was just sowing her gift.

While she was in her first year as the director of the toddlers ministry, I received a prophetic word for her. God said that He was paying close attention to how she stewarded this responsibility, because she wouldn't be able to enter the next phase of her ministry apart from faithfulness in her current position. I gave her the passage, "Do not despise these small beginnings, for the LORD rejoices to see the work begin" (Zechariah 4:10 NLT).

Many people never get to their destiny because they despised the day of small beginnings!

My wife tucked that word away in her heart and continued to serve out of love for the Lord and the toddlers. She would often spend ten hours preparing lessons for four-year-olds. She started getting creative ideas and enjoying it more and more. By the way, those who don't give it their best in their ministry, rarely enjoy it.

For three years she didn't receive much recognition or appreciation, but then, out of nowhere, the church asked her to join the pastoral staff, and today she is Pastor Meg. She has entered the next phase of her destiny. It's sad to think that many people never get to the next phase of their destiny because they despised the day of small beginnings!

Learn from Paul

Paul successfully lived out his destiny. He declared at the end of his life that he finished the race that God had set for him (2 Timothy 4:7). But it was before Paul was ever born that God destined for him to be an apostle to the Gentiles.

But when he who had set me apart before I was born, and who called me by his grace ...

—Galatians 1:15

Yet it was faithfulness that bridged Paul into his foreordained destiny. He writes:

And I thank Christ Jesus our Lord, who hath enabled me, for that he *counted me faithful*, putting me into the ministry.

—1 Timothy 1:12 KJV

When God led Paul into a season of deep prayer and study in the desert, Paul was very faithful. When God led Paul to serve as an assistant pastor at the church of Antioch, he was exceptionally faithful. It was only after he faithfully served in the seemingly less significant roles that he was released to take on his pre-destined apostolic ministry, which would shake the world!

In the church at Antioch there were prophets and teachers: Barnabas, Simeon called Niger, Lucius of Cyrene, Manaen (who had been brought up with Herod the tetrarch) and Saul. While they were worshiping the Lord and fasting, the Holy Spirit said, "Set apart for me Barnabas and Saul for the work to which I have called them." So after they had fasted and prayed, they placed their hands on them and sent them off.

—Acts 13:1-3 NIV

MANY ARE CALLED, FEW ARE COMMISSIONED

Many have been given great callings, but not many are faithful enough to be commissioned by God to enter into their callings.

Before Jeremiah was formed in his mother's womb, God had already crafted a destiny for him. Then there came a point in time when God released him into that great calling (see Jeremiah 1).

Paul was *called* before he was born but it wasn't until Acts 13 that he was *commissioned* by God to be released into his destiny! Faithfulness was the bridge that took Paul from just being a man with a great calling, to a man appointed, ordained, and commissioned into that great calling!

King David was called to be king as a little boy, but it was only after years of training and serving under King Saul that he was commissioned to be king. As a young man, David was even anointed to be king by Samuel the prophet, but he was appointed at a later time. Many are called and anointed, but few are commissioned and appointed. Those who are God-commissioned and God-appointed will always have a lot more fruit than those who are self-commissioned and self-appointed.

Some think that their destinies ought to be handed to them on a silver platter, just because they know that they have been called to greatness and they have an anointing. Do you know you are called to greatness? Good. Are you anointed? Good. Now faithfully serve where God has assigned you, and you will be among the few released into destiny. Many are *called*, but few are faithful and humble enough to be *commissioned*.

BURNING BRIDGES & BLAMING GOD?

You might be mad at God, saying, "I know you called me to do ... but nothing is working for me. I only have closed doors, and no one recognizes the gifts and callings that are upon my life. Maybe I should just give up on the dreams You gave me! I'm unfulfilled! I'm lost, and it's Your fault!"

God responds by asking you, "When I called you to the wilderness of My choice... the training camp of My choice... the Eli and Naomi that I put in your life and the smaller assignments I gave you... were you faithful? You have burned your own bridges to your destiny, and now you are blaming Me?"

There is no way around faithfulness and servanthood. Yes, your destiny is great, but greatness is only achieved through servanthood. Jesus said, "The greatest among you shall be your servant" (Matthew 23:11).

To walk into your destiny, you need to be appointed or promoted by God. Promotion comes only from God so you don't have to suck up to people. Just be obedient to God.

> For promotion cometh neither from the east, nor from the west, nor from the south. But God is the judge: he putteth down one, and setteth up another.
>
> —Psalm 75:6-7 KJV

God has already determined that it's a person of servanthood and faithfulness that He will promote. This might not be how it works in Hollywood or corporate America, but this is how it works in the kingdom of God. As a kingdom citizen, your destiny can only be achieved by kingdom principles. Thus, apart from faithful servanthood where God has currently assigned you, those big

God-given dreams will remain frustrating fantasies, and you will continually be lost and unfulfilled.

To desire promotion is not wrong in itself (see 1 Timothy 3:1). Just don't strive to be a faithful servant because you want to be promoted into greatness. Rather, let it be because you have a sincere love for God, and you are growing in intimacy with Jesus, the Greatest Servant ever to walk this earth. It's because you are being cultured by the kingdom of God, and you are peeling off the worldly mindsets, which seek to be catered to. May it be because you are beginning to see people as God sees them. You see, faithfulness and servanthood are not just outer acts but inner attitudes of the heart, requiring the right motive of pure love.

WHAT IF I GOT OFF COURSE?

Perhaps the last two chapters have been difficult for you because you realize where your assigned training camp was and you know you have failed there. Maybe you also recognize who your Eli and Naomi were and you feel convicted because you walked in dishonor and blew your goodbye kiss.

What now?

Before we tackle that question, let's get one thing straight: If you want to live out your God-given destiny, you can't choose your home church and tell God how you prefer to serve Him there. You have to let Him order your steps.

YOU DON'T PICK YOUR CHURCH

As Spirit-led people, the Lord must order the church we are planted in. I hate to break it to you, but none of us can change the world by ourselves; we need to work together with a team – a family.

God knows which team or family you will thrive the most in. If you don't believe that you need to be planted in a church fellowship, you are as lost as an amputated finger. How can an amputated part of the body fulfill its destiny? Impossible.

God knows in which local church body He can do the deepest work in you. God told Jeremiah, "Arise, and go down to the potter's house, and there I will let you hear my words" (Jeremiah 18:2). Wait a minute; if Jeremiah was already a prophet who was accurately hearing from God, why did he have to go to a certain house to have God speak to him? Couldn't God just speak to him where he was? There is a certain house (church body) that God will send you to because that's where He wants to speak to you and mold you for your destiny.

Some Christians have been saved for many years but because they refuse to go to their God-ordained potter's house, their lives look like ugly, unrefined blobs.

You don't pick your pastor because he's nice; you get planted with a church, ministry, and pastor according to God's orders.

> God settles the solitary [the lonely individual] in a home [family]; he leads out the prisoners to prosperity, but the rebellious dwell in a parched land.
>
> —Psalm 68:6, emphasis mine

Notice that God is the One who does the setting. In His matchless wisdom, He will station you in a church home that He sees is the best fit for you.

God knows His purposes for you, so trust that He's smart enough to put you in the right training center, or the right home church. If you want to rebel and reject the family to which God has sent you, you will have an unfruitful life and may die in the wilderness with an unfulfilled destiny.

Where is the church family in which God has set you? That's your training ground, your Eli, your Naomi.

LEFT PREMATURELY?

The late Kenneth Hagin's life and ministry impacted millions of lives around the world. If there is anyone in the last century who successfully walked out his or her destiny, you'd think he would be one of them. Yet, there was a time when he, too, missed God. He knew that God had ultimately called him into a traveling ministry, but he missed God's timing and prematurely left his church, which was his wilderness, his Eli, his Naomi.

He spent a few years in the traveling ministry and saw a few good things happen here and there, but he knew in his heart of hearts that something was off. He couldn't shake off the sense that God wasn't finished with him at his last church. This nagging discomfort, which was really sensitivity to the Holy Spirit, drove him to prayer where God made it clear to him that he was to return to his former church. Although he didn't like anything about the city where that church was located, he still obeyed. Since God is all-wise, this proved to be the best move that Hagin could have possibly made in relation to his destiny. At that church, he was further trained before God sent him out into his destiny as a traveling minister and the founder of Rhema Bible Training Center, where over 30,000 ministers have been trained.

In his excellent book, *Following God's Plan for Your Life,* Hagin explains it like this:

Because we had left that church prematurely the first time, God wasn't able to accomplish what He wanted to. But as a result of our obedience to go back there, God was able to teach me how to develop that congregation spiritually more than any other church we ever pastored. We learned many valuable lessons there. God's way is always the best![6]

If Kenneth Hagin had refused to back up to where he missed it, I doubt he would have been able to walk in the fullness of God's plan for His life.

Do you need to back up to where you missed it?

THE HOLY SPIRIT IS YOUR GPS

Have you left somewhere, someone, or something prematurely? Have you missed God?

If you get off course because you refused to listen to your GPS system, your GPS is kind enough to direct you back to wherever you need to be. The Holy Spirit is our GPS. He knows where God ultimately wants you, and He knows where you are right now. So even if you got off course, if you are willing to tune into His guidance again, He will get you back on track!

In Hagin's case, that meant returning to the church he had prematurely left. I can't say for certain that is what you need to do. But what I *do* know is that the Holy Spirit will get you back on track as long as you are willing to follow Him again! He is your Destiny Coach. The Father designed your destiny, the Son purchased your destiny on the cross, but it's the Holy Spirit who will navigate you into your destiny.

[6] Kenneth E. Hagin, *Following God's Plan for Your Life* (Kenneth Hagin Ministries, September 1993), 76-77.

I'm not saying that what Hagin did is what you need to do, but maybe it is. Maybe you need to apologize and reconnect with your Eli or Naomi; let the Holy Spirit speak to you about this. Remember, He might tell you to do the opposite of what your pride tells you to do. It may be humbling to admit that you were wrong and pick up where you left off, but if that's the bridge God wants you to cross to get into your destiny, don't despise that bridge! There may not be another one.

Maybe you're thinking, "I don't care if God tells me to go back to … I'm never going back!" With that kind of attitude, God cannot use you to do anything worthwhile for His glory. That attitude will cause you to grow spiritually deaf. When did you become the King of kings and Lord of lords? If you want to be that stubborn, you are foolishly sacrificing your destiny on the altar of stupidity.

But if you are willing to humble yourself to do whatever the Holy Spirit leads you to do, you will be overtaken by the wave of God's grace, and you will ride that wave into your destiny, for "God opposes the proud, but gives grace to the humble" (James 4:6).

Your situation may make it impossible for you to reconnect with your divine connection, for one reason or another (your pride does not count as one of them). It's OK; the Lord will lead you from where you are into your destiny. What's important is that you have a willing heart. As long as we have a willing heart, the Holy Spirit is our GPS.

You're Running Out of Gasoline

Someone may think, "I know what God wants me to do but I'm not going to do it! And since God already ordained my destiny and His gifts and callings are without repentance (see Romans 11:29), I'm sure I will still be able to fulfill my destiny."

It's true that God will not recall your destiny. He will not pull the plug on your gifts. He will not cancel your calling. But while our destiny, gifts, and calling don't die – we do.

Let me explain.

If someone gets off course for fifty years and then finally gets back on course by the grace of God, he or she will probably run out of gasoline without reaching their destination or fulfilling their full destiny.

Your destiny doesn't run out of gas, but you do. Every day that goes by means there is a little less fuel left in these earthly vehicles. So, you can hold onto your rebellion and miss the fullness of your destiny. The irony of holding onto sin is that it's really holding onto us, keeping us from fulfilling our destiny. Sin literally means to miss the mark. The mark is your God-ordained destiny.

Some of us like to think in terms of *someday* or *one day*. We may think, "Someday, I will be used by God powerfully" or "One day, I will know God intimately." But what we actually do *everyday* is more important than what we hope will happen someday or one day. I'm not saying that positive expectation is irrelevant, for we all ought to be people of vision. Yet, if we don't surrender to God today and everyday, will we really be able to walk into all God has prepared for us in the future? Why should God entrust us with something spectacular in the *future* if we undermine the only day that's currently entrusted to us: our today. Honor the Lord with your today by living surrendered to Him.

Surrender to the Lord again *today*. Tune in to your Holy Spirit GPS *everyday* and do whatever He says. You have no more gasoline to waste!

DESTINY QUESTIONS

1. Who is your David? (Someone whom God has brought into your life to minister to you.)

2. Who is your Eli? (Who is the person or where is the place that God has called you to assist in this season of your life?)

3. What are some of the weaknesses of your Eli that you do not want to duplicate? What are some of the things you want your Eli to impart to you?

4. Is there anything over which God has given you stewardship that seems very insignificant and small? Are you doing it with excellence, or slacking off?

5. Who or where is your Naomi that God has called you to be faithful to in rain or shine? (It can very well be the same as your Eli.)

6. Have you prematurely left a place that God has assigned you? If so, what does the Holy Spirit want you to do about this? (It might be a little different than what your pride wants to do.)

CHAPTER SIX

What Leads You?

Imagine that you need to drive across the country to get to a very important meeting. You look up the address of your destination and insert the address into your GPS system, but soon afterward, you throw the GPS out the window! What good is it to know *where* you are going if you don't know *how* to get there? That's as foolish as daydreaming about going to heaven without knowing how to get there (through faith in Christ).

Once, our friend, Stacy, was trying to get to her favorite restaurant. Others had driven her there many times, so she figured that she could find it on her own. She ended up lost and thirty miles away from her destination! If she had used a GPS, that wouldn't have happened. She knew *where* she was going but didn't now *how* to get there. It's not enough to know the final address of your destination or destiny. It's not enough to know where you are going; you need to know how to get there or else you will be lost. You need to be continually led by the Holy Spirit, who is our GPS.

Maybe God has revealed your destiny to you. Perhaps through a prophetic word you got a taste of your destiny. Maybe He has even taken you there in powerful dreams and visions. But if you throw out daily fellowship with the Holy Spirit, you will not get to your destination.

I'm all for prophetic words, dreams, and visions through which God can give us exciting snapshots of our future. But they are only addresses of our destination. We still need to learn to drive in sync with the Holy Spirit if we are to arrive at our appointed purpose.

How many Christians absolutely know what their destiny is? Now, how many Christians live being led by the Holy Spirit into fulfilling their destinies? It's even more important to be led by the Spirit than to know your destiny. What good is it if the most famous and accurate prophet gives a thirty-minute prophecy about your destiny, but you still don't know how to get there?

If God's people would learn to walk out their destiny, the world would become a much better place. The reason the kingdom of darkness has such a grip on earth is not because Jesus didn't do His part; it's that we haven't done *our* part to live out our destiny!

LED BY A PROPHET'S WORDS?

"For all who are led by the Spirit of God are sons of God" (Romans 8:14). The Scriptures don't tell us that we are to be led by prophecies, dreams, visions, or even common sense but, rather, the Holy Spirit. I'm not saying that the Holy Spirit can't use those mediums; but when Christians use those sources apart from being personally led by the Holy Spirit, it is very sad and unbiblical.

Let me explain.

Some have their ears perked up to hear a new prophetic word from a superstar prophet, but they don't know how to hear God for themselves. If we are led by prophetic words from a prophet, we better be sure to get their phone number and e-mail address, because we will need to get in touch with them to tell us what do next. I'm being sarcastic to make the point.

Scripture teaches that prophetic words are to be tested but not despised. "Do not despise prophecies, but test everything; hold fast what is good" (1 Thessalonians 5:20-21). Some take prophetic words too lightly, while others go overboard by not testing the prophetic word with the Scriptures and the indwelling Spirit. We are to carefully discern what God says to us instead of swallowing every "prophetic word" without bringing our Counselor, the Holy Spirit, into the conversation.

The seven churches in the book of Revelation (Revelation 2-3) all received prophetic words straight from Jesus Christ Himself through the apostle John. Imagine how weighty those prophetic words are; they are even archived in our Scriptures! Yet after each of those seven prophetic letters, Jesus closed by saying, "He who has an ear, let him hear what the Spirit says to the churches." Jesus didn't want them to just depend on prophetic words, but to really tune in to what the Spirit is saying in their spirit about the church. Most of these churches were so spiritually deaf that the only way they could hear from God was through a prophetic word. May that not be said of us!

One primary function of a personal prophetic word is to confirm what God has already spoken to you, personally. If it's something you've not heard from the Lord yet, go spend time with the Holy Spirit and ask Him if that prophetic word was from Him and what you should do with it.

After I officially joined Blessed International Fellowship, the pastor prophesied that I was to pursue full-time pastoral ministry. I didn't want to. At the young age of 21, I already felt like a big failure in pastoral ministry, and everyone I personally knew in full-time pastorates struggled financially, which caused strain in their families.

I was pursuing a degree at my university so I could be a high school history teacher. At best, I figured that I'd do some preaching on the side. But I took this prophetic word to prayer because we are not to despise prophetic utterances (see 1 Thessalonians 5:20).

I kept asking the Lord, "Is it full-time or part-time? Should I be a tent maker like Paul was for a period of his life, or should I just leap out in faith and pursue full-time ministry?" One morning, as I was in prayer, I fell into a trance. In this powerful experience, the Holy Spirit took me around the world and spoke to me in a piercing way, saying, "Even full-time ministry is not enough time to reach the harvest fields of the world!" I knew what God wanted me to do. Not because I had a trance – even drug addicts have visions – but because I heard the Holy Spirit speak to me. The Holy Spirit bore witness in my spirit as to what I needed to do.

LED BY ANY DREAM OR VISION?

We tend to be awed by the more spectacular ways that God grabs our attention, but let's make sure we don't undermine His still, small voice in our spirit.

The Holy Spirit can and does speak to us through dreams and visions, but these in themselves aren't what we base our decisions upon. I know a person who had a dream that her home church didn't want her anymore. She took this as a directional word from God and left the church. She had been doing great and growing spiritually while serving at her church, but after she left she started struggling in every area of her life. The pastoral staff told her that, based on that one dream, leaving the church was not the best decision for her to make; she disagreed. That particular dream was not a directional word from God, but only the surfacing of her own insecurities.

I know another woman who had a number of dreams in which she saw herself married to a certain man at the same church. He was clearly not interested in her, but she continued to believe it was God's will for them to get married. She continually stalked him, scaring the poor guy. Those dreams were not from the Holy Spirit; they came from her flesh, or maybe the pizza in her flesh! Yes, the Holy Spirit can speak directionally to you through dreams, but you must be led by *Him*, not by any dream or vision.

It is possible that Satan can send a false prophet to give you an erroneous prophetic word. Satan can use your flesh to produce a wacky dream, and he can even send strange demonic visions in which you hear voices. But Satan can't imitate or interfere with the Spirit-to-spirit fellowship that you personally develop with the Holy Spirit! It's from this Spirit-to-spirit fellowship that we make our decisions!

> The Spirit himself *bears witness* with our spirit that we are children of God.
>
> —Romans 8:16

The Holy Spirit gives us the inward witness that we are saved and also a witness regarding the decisions we need to make. The inward witness means that you know that you know that you know something in your spirit by the Spirit.

Peter fell into a trance where God showed him a profound vision, but he didn't know what the vision meant. Have you ever been there?

> And while Peter was pondering the vision, the Spirit said to him, "Behold, three men are looking for you. Rise and go down and accompany them without hesitation, for I have sent them."
>
> —Acts 10:19-20

If you study all of Acts 10, you learn that after hearing clearly from the Holy Spirit, Peter knew exactly what that vision meant; he was not to despise the Gentiles, but rather reach them with the gospel! Peter's Spirit-to-spirit relationship with the Holy Spirit opened the doors for the gospel to reach the Gentiles! If Peter didn't have a Spirit-to-spirit relationship with the Holy Spirit, he would have misunderstood the vision and missed God. How edifying are your dreams and visions if you have no interpretation? Interpretation comes by hearing the voice of the Holy Spirit in your spirit.

Only born-again believers have the privilege of being led by the Spirit of God in the most personal way – Spirit-to-spirit!

Some may think they are spiritual because they got a prophetic word, dream, or vision. I don't want to minimize these things, but even pagan kings (Pharaoh, Nebuchadnezzar and Darius) have had prophetic words given to them and received supernatural dreams and visions. However, only born-again believers have the privilege of being led by the Spirit of God in the most personal way – Spirit-to-spirit!

Led by Common Sense?

Most levelheaded people are led by common sense. Yet the Bible does not teach that "those who are led by *common sense* are children of God" but rather, "For all who are led by the *Spirit of God* are sons of God" (Romans 8:14).

Lot was led by common sense and chose to make his home near Sodom, which appeared to be very beautiful and prosperous (see Genesis 13:9-12). But we see that Lot's move to Sodom caused him to lose the souls of his daughters and the very life of his dear wife. Common sense backfired!

Common sense is a useful tool but, ultimately, you are called to "Trust in the LORD with all your heart, and do not lean on your own understanding [or common sense]. In all your ways acknowledge him, and he will make straight your paths" (Proverbs 3:5-6, emphasis mine).

God told Isaac to stay in the land he was in, even though they were in the midst of famine. God explained to Isaac that if he would remain in that famine-ridden land, he would be extremely blessed (see Genesis 26:1-3). Does that make any sense?

Jesus told the men at the wedding in Cana to take jars of water to the headwaiter, because it would be turned into the choicest wine (see John 2:8). Does that make any sense?

Jesus told Peter to walk on water, because he was in for an amazing adventure (see Matthew 14:29). Does that make any sense?

Jesus told His fishermen disciples to cast their nets to the right side for the harvest of their lifetime, even though they had already fished all night – in all directions – with no success (see John 21:6). Does that make any sense?

Here's the point: at times, the leading of the Holy Spirit will violate your common sense! Reason being: God is a whole lot smarter than you are! But if you dare to step out and follow His lead, you will prosper in a recession, you will embark on exciting adventures, you will be intoxicated on the new wine of the Spirit, and you will see a harvest of souls for the kingdom of God!

My wife and I bought two round trip tickets to fly in for my sister-in-law's graduation. Common sense told us that we should go because we had just enough in our savings, and my sister-in-law could really use our love and support. Then, just a week before our scheduled trip, the Holy Spirit began to speak to me, saying, "Cancel that trip." We didn't get travel insurance so canceling our trip meant losing eight hundred dollars. Common sense says that you shouldn't throw away eight hundred dollars, especially if you're living off a small salary, which we were at the time. But I told my wife what I was sensing in my spirit, and she trusted my leadership. We cancelled our trip without knowing why. You might think that we were foolish; I don't – even eight *million* dollars is not worth missing God.

LED BY HURT FEELINGS?

As children of God, we are to be led by the Holy Spirit, not by hurt feelings. If Elisha had been led by hurt feelings, he would have never walked into his awesome destiny of operating with the double-portion anointing of Elijah. Time after time, Elijah acted rudely toward Elisha (see 2 Kings 2), but Elisha knew that Elijah was his divine connection, and he wasn't going to disconnect over petty offenses. If Elisha had quit, saying, "Elijah doesn't appreciate me, I'm going to find another prophet who will!" Elisha would have over-reacted himself out of his destiny!

I've seen many people leave the church and pastor that God had connected them to, because they felt under-appreciated or offended. If you are led by your emotions, you will miss out on the double-portion anointing that God wants to put on your life. This is serious.

I heard about a well-known leader who purposefully offended his employees, testing them to see if they were ready for promotion. He promoted those who had skin thick enough to make spiritual decisions, not emotional ones. Emotional roller coasters are not ready for increased responsibility.

Jesus told at least five hundred people to wait in the Upper Room for the Holy Spirit; so after ten days of waiting, why did only one hundred and twenty people remain? Where were the other three hundred and eighty? They missed God! Why? I'm quite sure some of them had their feelings hurt and took off. Others might have been offended at some of the decisions the leadership were making – such as appointing an apostle through the lottery system – and ditched the group. If hurt feelings serve as the captain of your ship, you are in trouble.

LED BY OPEN DOORS?

Other people make all their decisions based on open doors, or given opportunities. They think that God is behind every open door, when Satan could be setting them up. Paul wanted to see the Thessalonians but the door was closed. Who was behind the closed door? Satan.

> We wanted to come to you – I, Paul, again and again – but Satan hindered us.
>
> —1 Thessalonians 2:18

Yes, it's true that God opens and closes doors for His people (see Revelation 3:7), but it's also true that Satan can deceptively open doors to temptation and close doors to breakthroughs. I'm not trying to credit the devil with more power than he has, but my point is simply this: when you have a door of opportunity that is opened before you, discern the source! How do you do that? Let the Holy Spirit speak clearly to your spirit.

> **When you have a door of opportunity that is open before you, discern the source!**

I heard one minister humorously teach that if he was led by open doors, he would be married to five different women, be a worship pastor at seventy different churches, all while teaching at seven different Bible colleges and pastoring two hundred churches! He was simply saying that open doors aren't how we make decisions, but being led by the Spirit is!

LED BY BARKING DOGS?

I once heard a story about a Christian couple that was getting married even though, originally, the girl had not been interested in the guy whatsoever. But she challenged God to give her a sign, saying, "When he comes to pick me up for our date, if my dog doesn't bark, I'll take it as he's the one to marry." He arrived at her doorstep, and her dog didn't bark. That's not the New Testament way to make life decisions! If demons were able to enter pigs in the time of Jesus, can they enter dogs and keep them from barking? (Just a thought.) Yet, if you have a strong Spirit-to-spirit communication with God, Satan won't be able to imitate or interfere.

If you know your Old Testament, you might be thinking: "Didn't Eliezer do something similar when He asked God for a sign?"

> Then he prayed, "Oh Lord God of my master Abraham, give me success today, and show kindness to my master Abraham. See, I am standing beside this spring, and the daughters of the townspeople are coming out to draw water. May it be that when I say to a girl, 'Please let down your jar that I may have a drink,' and she says, 'Drink, and I'll water your camels too' – let her be the one you have chosen for your servant Isaac. By this I will know that you have shown kindness to my master."
>
> —Genesis 24:12-14

You might also remember that Gideon, too, asked God for a sign (see Judges 6:37), but Gideon and Eliezer were under an inferior, Old Testament covenant. We are New Testament believers who have received much greater privileges. And to whom much is given, much more is now required (see Luke 12:48). We must live at a higher standard. We have the joy of the indwelling Holy Spirit to lead us; we do not need to challenge God to give us a sign.

Wait, didn't they cast lots in the New Testament to find Judas' replacement (Acts 1:23-26)? Wasn't casting lots similar to asking God for a sign? Yes, but that was in Acts 1, which was before the coming of the Holy Spirit in Acts 2. After Acts 2, never again do we see them casting lots. Rather, we see the early church being led by the Holy Spirit and being incredibly effective and fruitful. Why settle for signs when you have the Holy Spirit? Being led by prophetic words, a random dream or vision, common sense, or signs doesn't require intimacy with God; being led by the Holy Spirit does.

It's not that God will never use signs to get our attention. I remember when I was in college, and I was having doubts about pursuing a particular girl named Meg. I was discouraged and ready to quit the chase when I saw a car pull up in front of me with the license plate: ♥MEGDAN. It freaked me out and then spoke loud and clear to me: Love Meg, Daniel! I had the privilege of marrying that pretty girl, and she's proved to be the best wife for me. I'm not sure if God sent that car or not; it's possible that He used that sign to grab my attention. But regardless the type of sign, as children of God, we still need to be led by the Holy Spirit.

LED BY AMBITION?

Let's not mistake human ambition for divine vision. God wants us to be impregnated by His vision for our lives, not selfish ambitions. The difference between ambition and God's vision is that one is born of the Holy Spirit, while the other isn't. Whatever is not from the Holy Spirit is from the flesh and "Those who are in the flesh cannot please God" (Romans 8:8).

One who is led by ambition thinks like this: "I will prove to those who belittled me that I have become somebody! I'm going to totally *outdo* so and so. I can do it so much better than him or her, let me give it a shot!"

However, one who is led by God's vision speaks like this: "This is what God wants to do through my life by His grace, I'm humbled and honored. Therefore, I will wholeheartedly do what God has called me to do."

When someone has unresolved hurts and harbors bitterness, they will be motivated by ambition. Those rejection issues will convert into pride issues. Simon the Sorcerer wanted to move in the anointing like Peter and John. But Peter told him:

You have no part or share in this ministry, because your heart is not right before God. Repent of this wickedness and pray to the Lord. Perhaps he will forgive you for having such a thought in your heart. For I see that you are *full of bitterness* and captive to sin.

—Acts 8:21-23 NIV

It's not wrong to desire the anointing, but Simon had the wrong motive of selfish ambition, due to bitterness in his heart. A bitter heart produces ambition that desires to prove itself to the world – especially to those who hurt them. Bitterness is an oil spill in the heart, polluting our heart's motives. Thus, bitterness translates into pride. Pride is a mother sin, producing many children.

Those led by ambition are led by greed, hurt, and pride. Those led by fleshly ambition will find themselves farther from their destiny, and their relationship with God will suffer as sin slashes away at them.

For where jealousy and selfish ambition exist, there will be disorder and every vile practice.

—James 3:16

Notice how selfish ambition is packaged with jealousy. Those who are led by ambition are never content; they are always jealous of what others have. They will never have a calm resolve and always lust for more influence, success, etc. Their ambition serves as an insatiable, bottomless pit.

Those led by God's vision are led by a servant's heart, love, and humility. They will be drawn closer to the Lord because they know that God's vision is impossible to fulfill without Him. As they cling to Him, they will find His grace with them every step of the way into their destiny. They will be content with what God has for them and continue their journey with peace in their hearts.

While God's vision for your life is wisdom from God, fleshly ambition is from the devil:

> But if you have bitter jealousy and selfish ambition in your hearts, do not boast and be false to the truth. This is not the wisdom that comes down from above, but is earthly, unspiritual, demonic.
>
> —James 3:14-16

What or who do we want to drive us? God's vision or human ambition? God or the devil? Out of all the driven people that are in the world, how many of them are fueled by God's vision for their lives? How many are just running on selfish ambition? God knows. I sincerely pray that we would run on the right fuel. Only being fueled by God's vision will get you into your God-ordained destiny. The other fuel will get you somewhere... but not where God wants you to go. So at the end, those who were possessed by selfish ambition may have millions of dollars in the bank, but their lives will be in disorder! But if we run with God's vision and heart, we qualify to experience "The blessing of the LORD [that] makes rich, and he adds no sorrow with it" (Proverbs 10:22)!

IT'S NOT A COMPETITION

Being fixated on how others run their race will only stir human ambition and cause anxiety.

> Therefore, since we have so great a cloud of witnesses surrounding us, let us also lay aside every encumbrance

and the sin which so easily entangles us, and let us run
with endurance the race that is set before us.

—Hebrews 12:1 NASB

According to that Scripture, a race has been set before us. That
race is your God-designed destiny. This is not a race in which you
are competing with others; it is a race that has been custom built for
you. If you only look at how well others run their race, you will be
distracted from what God has called you to do.

Here are some temptations that you can fall into when you forget your race is not a competition:

- He just bought a house; I better buy one, too.
- He just planted a church; I better plant one, too.
- She just wrote a book; I better write one, too.
- He just recorded an album; I better catch up and do one
  myself.
- She just started a business; I think it's my turn next!

Imagine being a student who has worked very hard on your final
project, which counts for seventy percent of your final grade. After
turning in your project, you find out that you did the wrong assignment! In fact, you did the project that was assigned to another class!
Something similar happens to many Christians who are too focused
on how well others are running their courses.

You don't need to compare yourself with another person. While
the servant who received five talents was considered faithful for
turning his five talents into ten, the servant who received only two
talents was also considered faithful for turning his two talents into
four. More than statistics and results, being faithful with what we
were entrusted is what ultimately counts.

Paul told his young protégé, Timothy: "Fulfill your ministry" (2 Timothy 4:5). Ministry is simply serving God through serving people. We are all called to ministry, but not the same ministry. We might find people with similar ministries to us, but we all have our unique ministry that we must fulfill, our own race to complete. And it's not a competition.

LED BY ANXIOUS FEELINGS?

Many make decisions based on anxiety. They are so anxious to get married that they end up marrying the wrong person. They are anxious to get a job so they settle for the wrong job. They are anxious to start a ministry and as a result, they get ahead of God. They are anxious to get rich so they make stupid decisions. Because they are anxious to tell someone off, they spit out poisonous words that can never be taken back. Holy Spirit is not leading when we are controlled by anxiety. Anxiety is fear and "God gave us a spirit not of fear but of power and love and self-control" (2 Timothy 1:7).

The Holy Spirit doesn't lead through insecure, fearful, worried, troubled, and anxious feelings, but rather through His divine peace.

> Do not be anxious about anything, but in everything by prayer and supplication with thanksgiving let your requests be made known to God. And the peace of God, which surpasses all understanding [common sense], will guard your hearts and your minds in Christ Jesus.
>
> —Philippians 4:6-7

This Scripture assures us that the peace of God, which goes beyond common sense, will guard your heart and mind. That Greek word *guard* speaks of a watchman on the wall that will alert the city of oncoming danger and will stay at peace when all is well.[7] Pay attention to your inner peace, which is your destiny's watchman.

The context of that verse explains that the peace of God will guard our hearts, minds, lives, and destinies *if* we are people of prayer. As we do our part, God does His. God's peace may say, "Proceed, for all is OK," or it might scream, "Stop, danger is ahead!" Don't make decisions based on anxiety. Instead, pray! Surrender your anxieties, cares, and worries to the Lord, "Casting all your anxieties on him, because he cares for you" (1 Peter 5:7).

THE UMPIRE

> And let the peace (soul harmony which comes) from Christ rule (act as umpire continually) in your hearts [deciding and settling with finality all questions that arise in your minds, in that peaceful state].
>
> —Colossians 3:15 AMP

Inward peace serves as a watchman but also as an umpire. An umpire will carefully watch every play and declare it to be "SAFE!" or "OUT!" Pay attention to the voice of the Umpire! It comes from the Spirit of Christ who lives in our spirits.

If something grieves your spirit, it can very well be the ripple effect caused by the hurt emotions of the indwelling Holy Spirit. He's saying, "OUT! I don't will it." He's saying, "FOUL BALL! You're headed in the wrong direction."

I clearly remember a time I said something negative about a brother and how sick to my stomach I felt afterward. It wasn't from the lunch I ate; it was from the Spirit. I knew that I knew that the

---

[7] Strong's Concordance, 5431, http://concordances.org/greek/5432.htm

Holy Spirit didn't like my comment. Pay attention to His emotions in your spirit.

If something causes joy to bubble up in your spirit, it can very well be that your spirit detects the indwelling Holy Spirit dancing for joy. Jesus was sensitive to this, and by sensing the joy of the Holy Spirit, Jesus discerned the Father's will. He knew what was "SAFE" and what was a "HOME RUN!"

> In that same hour *he rejoiced in the Holy Spirit* and said, "I thank you, Father, Lord of heaven and earth, that you have hidden these things from the wise and understanding and revealed them to little children; yes, Father, *for such was your gracious will.*"
>
> —Luke 10:21

How Do We Stay Tuned In?

The keys to stay spiritually sensitive and tuned in to the voice of the Lord are worship and the Word of God. Worship and the Word will quiet the voice of anxiety, which compels us to make wrong decisions.

Let's look at worship: there is something about ministering to the Lord in worship that amplifies the voice of the Holy Spirit.

> While they were worshiping the Lord and fasting, the Holy Spirit said, "Set apart for me Barnabas and Saul for the work to which I have called them."
>
> —Acts 13:2

In worship, we give the Lord our attention. When you pay attention to someone, you tend to be more sensitive to him or her.

What Leads You?

When Elisha the prophet needed to hear from God, he called for a musician to come and play.

> "But now bring me a musician." And when the musician played, the hand of the LORD came upon him. And he said, "Thus says the LORD ..."
>
> —2 Kings 3:15-16

When the hand of the Lord came upon Ezekiel, he had powerful experiences with the voice of God. If you need a hand in making a decision, create an atmosphere of worship in you and around you, and you will know exactly what the Lord is saying.

Likewise, as you get into the Word of God on a daily basis, your spirit will be strengthened, and the voice of the Holy Spirit will grow stronger than the voice of your human intellect, fickle feelings, and bodily cravings. Our spirit is where the Holy Spirit resides. Thus, we want to make decisions based on the information we receive in our spirits, not our souls. Our soul consists of our mind, will, and emotions. Time spent in the Word of God helps us discern what is from our human soul and what the Spirit is showing our recreated spirit. Time in the Word will increase the volume of Spirit's voice, and other voices will fade.

> For the word of God is living and active, sharper than any two-edged sword, *piercing to the division of soul and of spirit*, of joints and of marrow, and discerning the thoughts and intentions of the heart.
>
> —Hebrews 4:12

When there is no blockage between our spirit and soul, the impressions of the Holy Spirit begin to flood over our souls. Spending time in the Word of God cuts out the blockage, enabling Holy Spirit revelation to flow into your soul! The Word is the only resource that's sharp enough to reach those hidden impediments. When they are removed, your mind begins to think the *thoughts* of God. Your emotions feel the *emotions* of God, and you will begin to desire the *will* of God.

When the Word clears the pores of our soul, His voice becomes stronger. After you take a nice hot shower, don't you feel more alert? It's because your pores have been cleared. When you spend time in the Word, you take a spiritual shower (John 15:3, Ephesians 5:26), and you will be a lot less sluggish when it comes to responding to the quickening of the Holy Spirit.

As I Pray, I Can't Shake Off the Sense That ...

As you seek to lead a Spirit-led life, pay attention to the impressions that you seem unable to shake off. When Peter was in prayer, three times he heard a voice say, "Take and eat" (see Acts 10:9-16). Not once, but thrice. Since Peter kept hearing the same thing, he had a difficult time shaking off this strong impression. People of prayer get strong impressions that they have a hard time simply ignoring. So, as a person of prayer, who worships as a lifestyle and is devoted to the Word, the deep impressions you receive that are not easy to forget may very well be the Lord lobbying for your attention.

DESTINY QUESTIONS

1. What has God recently spoken to you Spirit-to-spirit? Are you willing to do it even though it may violate common sense?

2. Have you been doing something God has not called you to do, but you were anxious to do it? If so, what is the Holy Spirit instructing you to do now that you realize you have been out of step with God?

3. Is there anything you have a hard time shaking off your heart, which you suspect is born of God?

CHAPTER SEVEN

We Need Wisdom

Your destiny is like a custom-made house whose blueprints have been designed by God Himself. Our responsibility is to partner with the Lord to manifest those blueprints on earth. In heaven, God has established your destiny, but that doesn't mean it will be established on earth. This cannot be done apart from receiving wisdom from the Lord: "By wisdom a house is built, and by understanding it is established" (Proverbs 24:3).

By revelation, Moses knew how the tabernacle was supposed to look, but he didn't know how to practically manifest it on earth. Therefore, God teamed Moses with Bezalel, who had the spirit of wisdom (see Exodus 35:30-31). Moses knew what needed to be built, and Bezalel knew how to build it. By the Holy Spirit, you can see your destiny and also have the wisdom to bring it into earthly manifestation.

Jesus is your wisdom (see 1 Corinthians 1:30). The Holy Spirit is the Spirit of Wisdom (see Isaiah 11:2). You are in Christ, and the Holy Spirit is in you. Therefore, wisdom is in you, over you, around you, and with you. But are you taking advantage of it? Are you accessing it?

Wisdom Is the First Thing

Some may think they need more money, time, etc., but we really need more wisdom. Not human wisdom, but God's wisdom. If we receive wisdom, we'd know how to get money. King Solomon didn't get the prosperity first. He received wisdom first, and riches overtook him. A fool can accidentally get the money first and then squander it as quickly as he got it. (Ask someone who won the lottery and then went bankrupt.)

Money doesn't guarantee wisdom, but wisdom knows how to access a prosperous life. Solomon was known throughout the world for his excellence, prosperity, and wisdom (see 1 Kings 10:7). As representatives of the King of kings and those who are under a better covenant than Solomon, should we expect anything less for God's people?

Solomon went up to the bronze altar before the Lord in the Tent of Meeting and offered a thousand burnt offerings on it. That night God appeared to Solomon and said to him, "Ask for whatever you want me to give you." Solomon answered God, "You have shown great kindness to David my father and have made me king in his place. Now, Lord God, let your promise to my father David be confirmed, for you have made me king over a people who are as numerous as the dust of the earth. Give me wisdom and knowledge, that I may lead this people, for who is able to govern this great people of yours?" God said to Solomon, "Since this is your heart's desire and you have not asked for wealth, riches or honor, nor for the death of your enemies, and since you have not asked for a long life but for wisdom and knowledge to govern my people over whom I have made you king, therefore wisdom and knowledge will be given you. And I will also give you wealth, riches and honor, such as no king who was before you ever had and none after you will have." Then Solomon went to Jerusalem from the high place at Gibeon, from before the Tent of Meeting. And he reigned over Israel.

—2 Chronicles 1:6-13 NIV

God commended Solomon for asking Him for wisdom and not for money, honor, the death of his enemies, or even long life. Why? When we know how to receive wisdom from God, then money, honor, victory over the devil and demons (our true enemies), and long life will all come as by-products. Proverbs 4:7 says that wisdom is the principle thing, or the first thing, according to the Young's Literal Translation of that verse.

People usually want the money fast, honor right away, deliverance today, and health and healing immediately. Yet, God's Word tells us that wisdom is the principle thing; it's what we need first.

A Chinese proverb says, "Give a man a fish and feed him for a meal, teach him to fish and feed him for a lifetime." Getting a fish is a picture of getting lucky. Learning to fish is a picture of gaining the wisdom of God in your life.

She [Wisdom] is a tree of life to those who lay hold of her; those who hold her fast are called blessed.

—Proverbs 3:18, emphasis mine

Wisdom is personified as a tree, and trees bear fruit. You can get a snack through someone else's tree or you can nurture your own tree. Picking fruit from someone else's tree is a picture of getting lucky. To grow your own tree is a picture of growing in wisdom.

If we get money by accident, we can lose it just as quickly. If we obtain honor accidentally, we can lose it just as easily. If we have a demon cast out of us (apart from our growth in wisdom), we can be oppressed again. If we received a healing through another person's faith, we can get sick again.

But if we made money by the wisdom of God, we can make more money. If we obtain honor by the wisdom of God, we can become even more honorable. If, by wisdom, we are victorious over the devil and his temptations, we can win again and again. If we are healed and physically strengthened by wisdom, we can repeatedly win over sickness and fatigue. Luck will bail you out once or twice, but wisdom will work for a lifetime.

Luck or Wisdom

There was a time that I was oppressed by demons of fear. During this time, I had heart palpitations every night from stress, and I was always worried out of my mind. Then, in the midst of this torment, I received a random deliverance. I went to a Bible study, and when the anointed pastor laid his hands on me, the oppression immediately lifted! I drove home worshiping God. I felt like I was walking on heavenly clouds for about three days, then the oppression came right back! It was because I received deliverance apart from increasing in wisdom.

You might ask, "How did you break it off the second time?" The Holy Spirit, who is the Spirit of Wisdom (see Isaiah 11:2), took me to the story of David and Goliath (see 1 Samuel 17). He explained to me that although the stone from David's sling knocked Goliath down, David had to take the sword and cut off the head of the ugly giant so he would have no chance to make a comeback.

Then He graciously explained to me that when that man of God prayed for me, it was like a stone that hit the spirit of fear. The stone is a picture of the anointing and authority in the name of Jesus, the Rock of our salvation; while the sword is a picture of the Word of God. The Holy Spirit told me that I needed to get into the Word of God and confess and declare over and over that "God has not given us the spirit of fear, but of love, power, and a sound mind" (2 Timothy 1:7 NKJV).

> **Luck will bail you out once or twice, but wisdom will work for a lifetime.**

As I obeyed this word of wisdom, the spirit of fear left me for good! The first time I got free, it was by chance, and my luck lasted three days. The second time I was freed, it was by wisdom, and I've been walking in freedom ever since. Don't depend of luck; depend on the wisdom of God. Wisdom is the principle thing.

Favor Follows Wisdom

All of us could use more favor. The increase in favor equals the increase of influence. And when we increase in influence, we bring greater glory to God!

- The prophet Samuel increased in favor and was able to use his increasing influence to glorify God (see 1 Samuel 2:26).

- Jesus increased in favor and was able to use His increasing influence to glorify God (see Luke 2:52).

- The early church increased in favor and was able to use their increasing influence to glorify God (see Acts 2:47).

- While favor brings influence, it's wisdom that brings favor.

- A servant who deals wisely has the king's favor (Proverbs 14:35).

- If you work for a king or a CEO, and you have the wisdom of God operating in your life, you will win favor. Favor spells promotion.

- The words of a wise man's mouth win him favor (Ecclesiastes 10:12).

- When you have the wisdom of God operating in your life, you will know what to say, and your words will bring you favor.

- Good understanding produces favor (Proverbs 13:15).

When you have the understanding that comes from God's wisdom, it will convert into favor. So what you really need is not a promotion, favor, or luck. You need wisdom from God. Wisdom brings favor. Favor brings influence. Influence enables you to glorify God. So don't you desire to grow in wisdom?

WISDOM SOLVES PROBLEMS

Wisdom does more than just bring (1) prosperity, (2) honor, (3) victory over devils, (4) health and long life, and (5) favor, influence, and greater glory to God. Wisdom from God also enables us to solve problems!

The early church was in a great dilemma. Satan was at work behind the scenes to create a church split and destroy the destiny of the Church. Two groups violently bumped heads – the Greek-speaking Jews and the Hebrew-speaking Jews – but by the wisdom of God, the apostles solved this problem by electing deacons.

> In those days when the number of disciples was increasing, the Grecian Jews among them complained against the Hebraic Jews because their widows were being overlooked in the daily distribution of food. So the Twelve gathered all the disciples together and said, "It would not be right for us to neglect the ministry of the word of God in order to wait on tables. Brothers, choose seven men from among you who are known to be full of the Spirit and wisdom. We will turn this responsibility over to them and will give our attention to prayer and the ministry of the word." This proposal pleased the whole group. They chose Stephen, a man full of faith and of the Holy Spirit; also Philip, Procorus, Nicanor, Timon, Parmenas, and Nicolas from Antioch, a convert to Judaism. They presented these men to the apostles, who prayed and laid their hands on them. So the word of God spread. The number of disciples in Jerusalem increased rapidly, and a large number of priests became obedient to the faith.
>
> —Acts 6:1-7

WISDOM PREVENTS OVER-REACTING

The twelve apostles could have overreacted to the situation and said, "Oh no, poor little babies, we will spend all of our time changing your diapers. We will take care of you." Instead, they responded wisely, without overreacting.

Whenever there is a problem, there is the temptation to overreact. Examples of overreaction would be:

- You have a bad experience with church so you never go to church again.

- Your boss hurts your feelings and you get so angry that you quit your job before God's timing.

- You tried something in business and it failed so you decide to never try that again.

- Maybe you had a problem with being religious in a negative way but then you go from being legalistic to licentious, and live without self-control! Or vise versa.

Don't you see why we desperately need wisdom?

Have you ever overreacted? If you are a basketball player who always hits the right side of the rim and you overreact in fleshly frustration so that you continually hit the left side of the rim, you went from one problem to another. You are still missing it! The wisdom of God will enable you to respond to problems with precision and not jump from one extreme to another, one problem to another.

WISDOM DISCERNS PRIORITIES

The Apostles knew how God wanted them to use their time. They knew they would waste their time if they waited on the tables; they were acutely aware that God called them to spend time in prayer, study of the Word, and teaching.

We either waste our time, or invest it. They knew what they needed to focus on. They knew how to discern the seasons of their lives. When you maximize each season of your life, you maximize your destiny! What does God want you to focus on right now? What does God want you to devote your time to? When you learn this, you don't just count the days, you make every day count!

So teach us to number our days that we may get a heart of wisdom.

—Psalm 90:12

Look carefully then how you walk, not as unwise but as wise, making the best use of the time, because the days are evil. Therefore do not be foolish, but understand what the will of the Lord is.

—Ephesians 5:15-17

We all have 24 hours in a day, so how should we manage our time? This takes the wisdom of God. Not everything we do is of equal importance. Do we know how to prioritize? By God's wisdom, we can.

When you know what God wants to focus on during this season of your life, and you do it, you will find God's grace to help you. God's grace speaks of His empowerment and favor. His grace is hidden in His will. Find what God wants you to do right now and His grace will be abundant for that task. That is how Paul was able to do so much work for God; he found God's grace behind him as he discerned what God wanted him to focus on and just did *that*. Paul wrote, "I worked harder than any of them, though it was not I, but the grace of God that is with me" (1 Corinthians 15:10).

WISDOM CASTS VISION

After the Apostles told the church what they decided to do, everyone responded favorably. That's a miracle! Just earlier, they wanted to rip out each other's hair. Now they are joining hands and jumping for joy. It takes wisdom to be a peacemaker, but it also takes wisdom to be a vision caster. In this passage, the Apostles cast the vision and everyone celebrates the vision and jumps on board.

What God has called you to do is so big that you will need to get other people on board to support the vision. What if you have a real vision from God, but everyone thinks your vision is cheesy and impossible? How are you going to get them as excited about it as you are? It takes the wisdom of God. A good leader knows how to cast vision. But casting vision must be done with godly wisdom for it to be successful!

WISDOM BRINGS SOULS INTO THE KINGDOM

The decision of the Apostles ultimately brought revival! We see that sinners became disciples – not church goers, but true disciples! We also see that priests became obedient to the faith. The priests were the kingpins of their day. A kingpin is the central pin in a bowling pin arrangement. When it falls, it has the greatest effect on the other pins. Therefore, kingpins are the most influential people of society. They are people of influence. Imagine seeing the most influential people on earth come to faith in Jesus. As we receive wisdom from God and do what He has called us to do, we will see disciples made and kingpins saved!

Recently, I heard someone say that if we truly believed in the severity of hell, we'd all quit our jobs and holler at the top of our lungs on the street corners. I disagree. The disciples were fishing all night and caught nothing until they received a word of wisdom from Jesus.

> He said to them, "Cast the net on the right side of the boat, and you will find some." So they cast it, and now they were not able to haul it in, because of the quantity of fish.
>
> —John 21:6

The way we will catch the most souls for the kingdom of God is to receive a word of wisdom from the Master and act accordingly. It's not doing open-air preaching for 26 hours a day. (I know there are 24 hours in a day, I'm being sarcastic to prove an important point.)

The way we will catch the most souls for the kingdom is to receive a word of wisdom from the Master and act accordingly.

I remember when I didn't know this; I would preach for hours on the street and pray for anyone and, pretty much, everyone. I'd go on dates with my wife, and she'd find that I had slipped away to pray for someone or witness. I'm all for having compassion for souls, but we will reach the most if we all just receive wisdom from the Lord. Proverbs 11:30 (NIV) tells us, "He who wins souls is wise." It takes wisdom to win souls.

The disciples were fishing all night and working hard. But when they got a word from Jesus, they began to work smart. Hard workers aren't always smart workers. There is such a thing as zeal without wisdom (see Romans 10:2), but we want both to converge in our lives. The hard worker will swing at the tree all day and night, using his dull axe. A smart worker will sharpen the axe. In other words, get wisdom from God, and do what He says.

Using a dull ax requires great strength, so sharpen the blade. That's the value of wisdom; it helps you succeed.

—Ecclesiastes 10:10 NLT

A review of the ten effects of wisdom that we have just covered:

1. Prosperity

2. Honor

3. Victory over devils

4. Health and long life

5. Favor, influence, and greater glory to God

6. Ability to solve problems

7. Prevention from overreacting

8. Enables to discern priorities

9. Empowers the leader to cast vision

10. Wins souls into the kingdom of God

~FIVE KEYS TO GROW IN WISDOM~

1. DON'T DEPEND ON HUMAN WISDOM

Solomon didn't settle for human wisdom. He didn't rely on his life experiences and education; he longed for divine wisdom. When you depend on human wisdom, you disqualify yourself from God's wisdom. Another name for human wisdom is common sense. Common sense can be a great tool, but it's greatly limited. Why should we trust in human wisdom when we are no longer just human? We are new creations who can access the wisdom of God!

> Trust in the LORD with all your heart, and do not lean on your own understanding. In all your ways acknowledge him, and he will make straight your paths.
>
> —Proverbs 3:5-6

If we ever depend on our human strength, we dam up the power of the Holy Spirit.

If we ever depend on our human strength, we dam up the power of the Holy Spirit. That is why the Scriptures tell us, "This is the word of the Lord to Zerubbabel: 'Not by might, nor by power, but by my Spirit, says the LORD of hosts'" (Zechariah 4:6). Once we trust in our might and power, we go without the help of the Spirit of the Lord. The same principle is true when applied to wisdom. If we depend on human wisdom, we silence the Spirit of Wisdom.

2. Continually Ask God for Wisdom

Solomon asked God for wisdom; he knew he needed it. The proof that you have a measure of wisdom is that you crave more of it. The fool is the one who doesn't seek wisdom, since he doesn't see his need for it.

The Scripture tells us that we have not because we ask not (see James 4:2). We need to ask God for wisdom on a regular basis. As you do, you may go into your prayer closet with confusion, but you will leave with clarity! You might come to Him with questions, but you will leave with answers! You might come into His presence feeling lost, but you will leave possessed by His purposes.

> If any of you lacks wisdom, he should ask God, who gives generously to all without finding fault, and it will be given to him. But when he asks, he must believe and not doubt, because he who doubts is like a wave of the sea, blown and tossed by the wind. That man should not think he will receive anything from the Lord; he is a double-minded man, unstable in all he does.
>
> —James 1:5-8 NIV

We have all experienced miserable, even humiliating, failures. That is when we especially need to receive wisdom from the Lord. When the disciples couldn't cast out a certain demon, they sought out Jesus privately, and He explained what they needed to do next time so they wouldn't fail again (see Matthew 17:20-21). When you present your failures before the Lord, He will do more than just tell you what you did wrong; He will tell you how to succeed next time. That's a great deal!

I find that many Christians have an area of weakness where they continually fail. They can have a pattern of failure in that specific area that has lasted for many years. They try everything they can to not fail again, but they simply can't walk in continual victory. That's when we have to come before the Lord, and ask Him to show us why we have failed in that area and what we need to do so that we will never fail again.

You can just try to follow the advice of others and, although their words might be well meaning and potentially helpful, what you really need is a customized prescription for your customized problem. God's wisdom can show you the root of the problem and even provide the very solution that will keep you from ever falling again into those besetting sins and habitual failures.

3. Worship & Wisdom

Solomon had just finished worshiping the Lord in the Tent of Meeting when the Lord asked Him what he wanted. Today we don't worship with blood sacrifices, but through our praises (see Hebrews 13:15). When you get lost in worship, you find His wisdom.

While Solomon only had wisdom resting *on* him, we, in the New Covenant, have the Spirit of wisdom *within* us. As we worship, that river of wisdom begins to flow from our spirits into our lives and then out into the world (see John 7:38)!

4. Seek Wisdom for the Sake of the Kingdom

Solomon desired wisdom so he could better serve the kingdom of Israel. His motive wasn't to be rich or famous, but to be a blessing. Now, we serve the kingdom of God. And for the sake of God's kingdom, the glory of our King, and the destruction of the kingdom of darkness, we ought to seek wisdom. The motive is not selfish ambition, but love. It's about His kingdom. "But seek first the kingdom of God and his righteousness, and all these things will be added to you" (Matthew 6:33).

The word of wisdom is one of the nine gifts of the Holy Spirit (see 1 Corinthians 12:8). We are commanded to "pursue love, yet desire earnestly spiritual gifts" (1 Corinthians 14:1 NASB). The key to operating the gifts of the Spirit is earnest desire. Yet, the reason for our desire of the word of wisdom is our love for King Jesus, His kingdom, and people.

5. INVEST IN WISDOM

In the book of Proverbs, Solomon encourages us to "buy wisdom" (Proverbs 23:23). If we desire to grow in wisdom, we need to do more than just ask God for it (although that is pivotal, as we already established). We also need to invest our time and money to grow in wisdom.

The spirit of wisdom is contagious and can be imparted. Moses laid his hands on Joshua and imparted the spirit of wisdom (see Deuteronomy 34:9). You can receive an impartation of wisdom as you spend time with men and women of God who have the Spirit of wisdom in a greater measure than you and as you serve their ministries (like Joshua did for Moses). This may mean reading their books, attending their conferences, partnering, volunteering, sowing financially, etc.

> Whoever walks with the wise becomes wise, but the companion of fools will suffer harm.
>
> —Proverbs 13:20

Wisdom doesn't come to the casual seeker, but to those who value it enough to buy it. I've spent an astonishing amount of money and time for the purpose of growing in wisdom. I don't plan to stop, and I don't regret it one bit because, as you can see from this chapter, wisdom is the principle thing. Apart from God's wisdom, we are lost, unfulfilled, and our glorious destiny becomes as unreachable as the sun.

Destiny Questions

1. Have you failed recently in an area of your life? Ask God why you failed and what you need to do so that you will never fail there again.

2. Do you crave wisdom? If so, what are you doing to buy wisdom?

For Further Study

Go to danielhpark.com
for many free resources and to see how you can
order other books and teaching CDs.

If you wish to dive deeper into the subject of destiny,
order the seven CD set,
Find & Fulfill Your God-Given Destiny,
from Daniel Park Publications.

Contact the author at:
PastorDHP@gmail.com

Never Burn Out!

Never Burn Out: discover the reality of your identity is written using practical, easy to understand illustrations that effectively communicate powerful truths that will bring a new, higher level of freedom to the life of the reader. The revelations found in the pages of this book will launch you into a thrilling, fulfilling, joyful life of never-ending revival.

Burn out is not an uncommon condition in this hour. Not only will this book give you keys to protect you or heal you from burn out it will also ground you in your God-given identity in Christ. Discovering who you are, will release the liberty and power of the Spirit in you to take the kingdom by force – to carry and release the glory of God everywhere you go!

This book is a "must read" for every believer who wants to experience the thrill of discovering their true identity in the Person of Jesus Christ.

—Dr. A.L. Gill—

To order copies of
Step Into Destiny
go to: danielhpark.com

Additional copies of this book and other book titles
from XP Publishing are available at
XPmedia.com

BULK ORDERS:
We have bulk/wholesale prices for stores and ministries.
Please contact: usaresource@xpmedia.com and the
resource manager will help you.
Our books are also available to bookstores through
Anchordistributors.com
For Canadian bulk orders, please contact:
resource@xpmedia.com

www.XPpublishing.com